D1369238

BASIC GRAMMAR

A · N · D

USAGE

THIRD
ALTERNATE
EDITION

PENELOPE CHOY
Los Angeles City College

JAMES McCORMICK
San Bernardino Valley College

Harcourt Brace Jovanovich College Publishers
Fort Worth   Philadelphia   San Diego   New York   Orlando   Austin   San Antonio
Toronto   Montreal   London   Sydney   Tokyo

Acquisitions Editor: Karen Allanson

Manuscript Editor: Karen Carriere

Production Editor: Pat Gonzalez

Designers: Kay Faust
Linda Cable

Production Manager: Mandy Van Dusen

Copyright © 1992, 1985, 1983, 1980, 1978 by Harcourt Brace Jovanovich, Inc.

All rights reserved. No part of this publication may be reproduced or transmitted in any form or by any means, electronic or mechanical, including photocopy, recording, or any information storage and retrieval system, without permission in writing from the publisher.

Permission is hereby granted to reproduce the Exercises in this publication in complete pages, with the copyright notice, for instructional use and not for resale by any teacher using classroom quantities of the related student textbook.

ISBN: 0-15-504937-2

Library of Congress Catalog Card Number: 89–81002

Printed in the United States of America

Preface

This book is an alternate version of the Third Edition of *Basic Grammar and Usage*. It retains the essential form of the earlier editions, but several improvements have been made. The first unit of the text, "Identifying Subjects and Verbs," which stresses the primacy of that skill, has been enlarged by a new lesson, "The Position of Verbals." The second unit on subject–verb agreement has been rearranged to bring like rules together. The final unit now includes an entirely new lesson on such matters as italics, colons, and quotation marks. All of the lessons have new expository material, new examples, and new exercises. This edition also adds ready-reference lists and charts of key material inside the front and back covers.

To make it possible for instructors to quickly reproduce Unit Tests, Diagnostic Tests, and Achievement Tests, the *Teacher's Manual* has been enlarged to an 8 1/2″ × 11″ format. And a brief introduction, with suggestions for using the text, has been added to the manual.

This edition was planned by Penelope Choy and James McCormick. Penelope Choy aided in the revision of Unit One. James McCormick revised the remainder of the text and the *Teacher's Manual*.

The authors are grateful to the following instructors for reviewing the second edition and for suggesting many of the revisions in this edition: Carol O. Sweedler-Brown (San Diego State University), Dennis Gabriel (Cuyahoga Community College), David Pichaske (Southwestern State University), and Gwen Rowley (Mesa Community College). We also thank Thomas Chamberlain and Leonard Lardy, friendly critics at San Bernardino Valley College.

We are grateful to many individuals at Harcourt Brace Jovanovich: Bill McLane, senior editor and gray eminence of this edition; Karen Allanson, acquisitions editor; Karen Carriere, manuscript editor; Pat Gonzalez, production editor; Mandy Van Dusen, production manager; Kay Faust, designer of our lovely new cover; and Linda Cable, project designer of this alternate edition.

We also thank, of course, our spouses, Gene and Virginia, who have kept a sense of humor.

Penelope Choy
James McCormick

Preface to the First Edition

Basic Grammar and Usage was originally written for students in a special admissions program at the University of California, Los Angeles. As part of their participation in the program, the students were enrolled in a composition and grammar course designed to prepare them for the university's freshman English courses. When the program began in 1971, none of the grammar textbooks then on the market seemed suitable for the students, whose previous exposure to grammar had been cursory or, in some cases, nonexistent. As the director of the programs's English classes, I decided to write a book of my own that would cover the most important areas of grammar and usage in a way that would be easily understood by my students.

The original version of *Basic Grammar and Usage* received an enthusiastic response from the students and was used successfully throughout the three-year duration of the program. After the program ended in 1974, many of the instructors asked permission to reproduce the book for use in their new teaching positions. By the time copies of *Basic Grammar and Usage* reached Harcourt Brace Jovanovich in 1975, the text had already been used by more than 1,500 students in nearly a dozen schools.

Basic Grammar and Usage presents material in small segments so that students can master a particular topic one step at a time. The lessons within each unit are cumulative. For example, students doing the pronoun exercises for Lesson 19 will find that those exercises include a review of the constructions treated in Lessons 16 to 18. This approach reinforces the students' grasp of the material and helps them develop the skills they need for the writing of compositions. To make them more interesting to students, the exercises in four of the six units are presented as short narratives rather than as lists of unrelated sentences. Each lesson concludes with two exercises, which may be either used in class or assigned as homework. In addition, each unit ends with a composition that the students must proofread for errors and then correct to demonstrate mastery of the material.

Students who have never before studied grammar systematically will find that working through the text from beginning to end provides an insight into the basic patterns of English grammar. As one student commented on an end-of-course evaluation, "The most important thing I learned from *Basic Grammar and Usage* is that if you learn what an independent clause is, half of your grammar problems are over." On the other hand, students who do not need a total review of grammar can concentrate on the specific areas in which they have weaknesses. To help the instructor evaluate both types of student, the Instructor's Manual accompanying the text includes a diagnostic test and a post-test divided into sections corresponding to the units in the book. There are also separate achievement tests for each unit, as well as answer keys to the exercises presented in the text.

Although *Basic Grammar and Usage* is designed for students whose native language is English, it has been used successfully by students learning English as a second language. In addition to being a classroom text, *Basic Grammar and Usage* can be used in writing labs and for individual tutoring.

Many people have shared in the preparation of *Basic Gramamar and Usage*. I wish in particular to thank the instructors and administrators of UCLA's Academic Advancement Program, where this book originated. In revising the text for publication, I have been greatly helped by the suggestions of Regina Sackmary of Queensborough Community College of the City University of New York and by Elizabeth Gavin, formerly of California State University, Long Beach, who reviewed the manuscript for me. Sue Houchins of the Black Studies Center of the Claremont Colleges contributed many ideas and reference materials for the exercises. An author could not ask for more supportive people to work with than the staff of Harcourt Brace Jovanovich. I owe a special debt of gratitude to Raoul Savoie, who first brought the UCLA version of the text to the attention of his company. I also wish to thank Lauren Procton, who was responsible for the editing, and Eben W. Ludlow, who has provided guidance and encouragement throughout all the stages of this book's development.

Penelope Choy

Contents

Preface   iii

Preface to the First Edition   v

UNIT ONE   Identifying Subjects and Verbs   1

    1 Sentences with One Subject and One Verb   1
    2 Multiple Subjects and Verbs   15
    3 Distinguishing Between Objects of Prepositions and Subjects   25
    4 Main Verbs and Helping Verbs   37
    5 The Position of Verbals   47
    Unit Review   57

UNIT TWO   Subject–Verb Agreement   59

    6 Recognizing Singular and Plural Subjects and Verbs   59
    7 Indefinite Pronouns as Subjects   71
    8 Subjects Understood in a Special Sense   79
    9 When Subjects Are Joined by Conjunctions (for parallel structure)   87
    Unit Review   95

UNIT THREE   Identifying and Punctuating the Main Types of Sentences   97

10 Compound Sentences   97

11 Complex Sentences   109

12 Compound–Complex Sentences, Comma Splices, and Run-On Sentences   121

13 Correcting Fragments   133

Unit Review   143

UNIT FOUR   Punctuation That "Sets Off" or Separates   145

14 Parenthetical Expressions   145

15 Appositives   157

16 Restrictive and Nonrestrictive Clauses   167

17 Items in a Series and Dates and Addresses   179

Unit Review   187

UNIT FIVE   Pronoun Usage   189

18 Subject, Object, and Possessive Pronouns   189

19 Pronouns in Comparisons and Pronouns with *-self, -selves*   201

20 Agreement of Pronouns with Their Antecedents   209

21 Order of Pronouns and Spelling of Possessives   221

Unit Review   229

**UNIT SIX   Capitalization, More Punctuation, Placement of Modifiers,
            Parallel Structure, and Irregular Verbs   231**

22 Capitalization   231

23 More on Punctuation   241

24 Misplaced and Dangling Modifiers   249

25 Parallel Structure   257

26 Irregular Verbs   265

Unit Review   271

Answers to "A" Exercises   275

Index   289

IDENTIFYING SUBJECTS AND VERBS

1

Sentences with One Subject and One Verb

The most important grammatical skill you can learn is how to identify subjects and verbs. Just as solving arithmetic problems requires you to know the multiplication tables perfectly, solving grammatical problems requires you to identify subjects and verbs with perfect accuracy. This is not as difficult as it sounds. With practice, recognizing subjects and verbs will become as automatic as knowing that $2 \times 2 = 4$.

Although in conversation people often speak in short word groups that may not be complete sentences, in written English people usually use complete sentences.

A complete sentence contains at least one subject and one verb.

A sentence can be thought of as a statement describing an *actor* performing a particular *action*. For example, in the sentence "The man fell," the *actor* or person performing the action is the *man*. What *action* did the man perform? He *fell*. This *actor—action* pattern can be found in most sentences. Can you identify the actor and the action in each of the sentences below?

The artist painted.
The audience applauded.

The *actor* in a sentence is called the **subject.** The *action* word in a sentence is called the **verb.** Together, the subject and verb form the core of the sentence. Notice that even if extra words are added to the two sentences above, the subject–verb core in each sentence remains the same.

The artist painted portraits of famous people.
At the end of the concert, the audience applauded loudly.

You can see that in order to identify subjects and verbs, you must be able to separate these core words from the rest of the words in the sentence.

Here are some suggestions to help you identify verbs.

1. The *action* words in sentences are verbs. For example:

The team *lost* the game.
I *play* tennis every weekend.
This bank *offers* high interest rates.

Underline the verb in each of the following sentences.

This restaurant serves low-sodium meals.

Dieters count calories.

The employees want higher salaries.

2. All forms of the verb *be* are verbs: *am, is, are, was, were,* and *been.* For example:

Sam *is* happy.
The patient *was* very weak.

Verbs also include words that can be used as substitutes for forms of *be,* such as *seem, feel, become,* and *appear.* These verbs are called **linking verbs.**

Sam *seems* happy
The patient *feels* very weak.

Underline the verb in each of the following sentences.

I am nervous about my new job.

Paula becomes nervous during job interviews.

The witness appeared nervous during the trial.

3. Verbs are the only words that change their spelling to show tense. **Tense** is the time – present, past, or future – at which the verb's action occurs. For example, the sentence "We *work* for United Airlines" has a present-tense verb. The sentence "We *worked* for United Airlines" has a past-tense verb. Underline the verb in each of the following sentences.

I enjoy good books.

My children enjoyed their trip to Disneyland.

Our class meets three days a week.

My sister met me at the airport.

The school needs more teachers.

The car needed a new battery.

Identifying verbs will be easier for you if you remember that the following kinds of words are *not* verbs.

4. An **infinitive** – the combination of the word *to* plus a verb, such as *to walk* or *to study* – is *not* considered part of the verb in a sentence. Read the following sentences.

The police tried to capture the robbers.
The airline wants to raise its fares.

The main verbs in these two sentences are *tried* and *wants*. The infinitives *to capture* and *to raise* are *not* included. Underline the main verb in each of the following sentences.

Stella hopes to become a movie star.

Congress voted to change the federal income tax system.

5. **Adverbs** – words that describe a verb – are *not* part of the verb. Many commonly used adverbs end in *-ly*. The adverbs in the following sentences are italicized. Underline the verb in each sentence.

The doctor examined the patient *carefully*.

The instructor *patiently* explained the lesson.

The dog barked *loudly*.

The words *not, never,* and *very* are also adverbs. Like other adverbs, these words are *not* part of the verb. Underline the verb in each of the following sentences. Do *not* include adverbs.

My husband never forgets our anniversary.

The traffic moved very slowly.

I exercise regularly.

Dinner is not ready yet.

The students quickly finished the exercises.

Now that you can identify verbs, here are some suggestions to help you to identify subjects.

1. The subject of a sentence is most frequently a noun. A **noun** is the name of a person, place, or thing, such as *Laura, Dallas,* or *pencils*. A noun may also be the name of an abstract idea, such as *happiness* or *success*. Underline the subject in each of the following sentences *once* and the verb *twice*. Remember that the verb is the *action,* and the subject is the *actor*.

Martha supports two children by herself.

The car hit a telephone pole.

California produces most of the nation's artichokes.

Alcoholism ruined his career.

2. The subject of a sentence may also be a **subject pronoun**. A **pronoun** is a word used in place of a noun, such as *she* (= *Laura*), *it* (= *Dallas*), or *they* (= *pencils*). The following words are subject pronouns:

I, you, he, she, it, we, they

Underline the subject in each of the following sentences *once* and the verb *twice*.

He started a new job yesterday.

It always rains during April.

Last month I moved to a new apartment.

They often argue about money.

She is my best friend.

3. In **commands**, such as "Shut the door!", the subject is understood to be the subject pronoun *you*, even though the word *you* is almost never included in the command. *You* is understood to be the subject of the following sentences.

Dial 911 in case of emergencies.
Please lower your voice.

Underline the subject in each of the following sentences *once* and the verb *twice*. If the sentence is a command, write the subject *you* in parentheses at the beginning of the sentence.

An earthquake shook the city.

Help me!

He jogs five miles every morning.

Clean the stove after dinner.

Identifying subjects will be easier for you if you remember that the following kinds of words are *not* subjects.

4. **Adjectives** – words that describe a noun – are *not* part of the subject. For example, in the sentence "The young actress won an Oscar," the subject is "actress," *not* "young actress." In the sentence "A private college charges tuition," the subject is "college," *not* "private college." Underline the subject in each of the following sentences *once* and the verb *twice*.

Tuna casseroles often appear at potluck dinners.

Microwave ovens shorten cooking time.

Hot fudge sundaes are my favorite dessert.

The new fall fashions include both long and short skirts.

5. Words that show **possession**, or ownership, are *not* part of the subject. Words that show possession include nouns ending in an apostrophe (') combined with *s*, such as *David's* or *car's*. They also include **possessive pronouns**, words that replace nouns showing ownership, such as *his* (= *David's*) or *its* (= *car's*). Possessive pronouns include the following words:

my, your, his, hers, its, our, their

Since words that show possession are *not* part of the subject, in the sentence "My daughter wears glasses," the subject is "daughter," *not* "my daughter." In the sentence "Judy's landlord raised the rent," the subject is "landlord," *not* "Judy's landlord." Underline the subject in each of the following sentences *once* and the verb *twice*.

Stuart's snores annoyed his roommate.

Our team scored two touchdowns in the fourth quarter.

Egypt's pyramids attract many tourists.

His friends gave him a surprise birthday party.

Here is a final suggestion to help you to identify subjects and verbs accurately.

Try to identify the verb in a sentence before you try to identify the subject.

A sentence may have many nouns, any of which could be the subject, but it will usually have only one or two verbs. For example:

> The theater in my neighborhood offers a special discount to students and senior citizens.

There are five nouns in the above sentence (*theater, neighborhood, discount, students, citizens*), any of which might be the subject. However, there is only one verb—*offers*. Once you have identified the verb as *offers*, all you have to ask yourself is, ''Who or what offers?'' The answer is *theater*, which is the subject of the sentence.

Identify the subject and verb in the following sentence, remembering to look for the verb first.

> These luxurious apartments appeal to people with high incomes and no children.

Remember these basic points:

1. The action being performed in a sentence is the **verb.**
2. The person or thing performing the action is the **subject.**
3. A sentence consists of an *actor* performing an *action*, or, in other words, a **subject** plus a **verb.**

Since every sentence you write will have a subject and a verb, you must be able to identify subjects and verbs in order to write correctly. Therefore, as you do the exercises in this unit, apply the rules you have learned in each lesson, and *think* about what you are doing. Do not make random guesses. Grammar is based on logic, not on luck.

Underline the subject in each of the following sentences *once* and the verb *twice*. Add the subject *you* in parentheses if the sentence is a command.

> That car costs too much for my budget.

> Her pink and purple hair attracted a lot of attention.

> Raw seafood sometimes contains harmful bacteria.

> The dog's constant barking disturbed the neighbors.

Keep an eye on the traffic.

Sturdy, reliable appliances no longer seem to exist.

Love is blind.

EXERCISE 1A

Underline each subject *once* and each verb *twice*. Each sentence has only one subject and only one verb. *Remember to look for the verb first* before you try to identify the subject.

1. Sir William Jones lived in India in 1786.

2. He decided to study Sanskrit.

3. Sanskrit was the ancient language of India.

4. Sir William made an amazing discovery.

5. Sanskrit strongly resembled two ancient European languages, Latin and Greek.

6. But India is in Asia.

7. And Europe was thousands of miles to the west!

8. Many basic Sanskrit words sounded nearly like Greek or Latin words.

9. One example is *pitar* in Sanskrit.

10. That word means "father."

11. The Latin word is *pater.*

12. Notice the similarity of *pitar* and *pater.*

13. *Matar* is Sanskrit for "mother."

14. The Latin word is **mater.**

Copyright © 1992 by Harcourt Brace Jovanovich, Inc. All rights reserved.

15. Jones discovered hundreds of resemblances in the three languages.

16. He decided to rule out coincidence.

17. Only one explanation seemed possible.

18. All three languages had a common source!

19. Later scholars confirmed Jones' idea.

20. They called the common source "Indo-European."

21. Evidently Indo-European was an oral language.

22. Many other modern languages come from the Indo-European language.

23. Indo-European's modern descendants include Iranian, Hindi, Pushtu, Russian, German, French, Spanish, Irish, and, last but not least, English.

Copyright © 1992 by Harcourt Brace Jovanovich, Inc. All rights reserved.

EXERCISE 1B

Underline the subject of each sentence *once* and the verb *twice*. Each sentence has one subject and one verb. *Remember to look for the verb first* before you try to locate the subject.

1. Marya Sklodowska began her life in Poland in 1867.

2. Her father taught high school physics and mathematics.

3. At that time Poland was under Russian domination.

4. Her outspoken father lost his job.

5. He was not sufficiently pro-Russian.

6. Marya's oldest sister died of typhoid fever.

7. Her mother died of tuberculosis in 1878.

8. Marya saw science as the answer to poverty and disease.

9. She decided to become a scientist.

10. She won a gold medal as the top graduate of her high school.

11. Her oldest sister wanted to go to Paris to study medicine.

12. Poland had no college programs for women.

Copyright © 1992 by Harcourt Brace Jovanovich, Inc. All rights reserved.

13. Marya took four years of low-paying jobs to support her sister's studies in Paris.

14. She took secret science classes at night to avoid the authorities in Poland.

15. Finally Marya moved to Paris to begin college.

16. She studied obsessively to catch up with the French students.

17. Marya married a French physicist, Pierre Curie.

18. She became Marie Curie.

19. The Curies received the Nobel Prize in 1903 for their discoveries in radioactivity.

20. Marie won another Nobel Prize in 1911 for her work in chemistry.

21. She was the first scientist ever to win two Nobel Prizes.

Copyright © 1992 by Harcourt Brace Jovanovich, Inc. All rights reserved.

EXERCISE 1C

Each group of words below can be made into a complete sentence by the addition of *one* word. The missing word may be a subject (a noun or a subject pronoun) or it may be a verb. Make each group of words a sentence by adding either a *one-word subject* or a *one-word verb*.

1. _____ was her best friend.

2. My sister's _____ was a present.

3. Every word _____ at least one vowel.

4. His _____ cost forty-two dollars.

5. Last week Mary _____ from high school.

6. His _____ meets on Tuesdays.

7. They _____ the car in two days.

8. Johnny's house _____ a white fence.

9. That new mall _____ last month.

10. Lavonne _____ in a beauty parlor.

11. _____ is his favorite pastime.

12. His older _____ dates a friend of mine.

13. The teacher's _____ was in the front of the room.

14. The old, gray _____ slowly sank under the waves.

Copyright © 1992 by Harcourt Brace Jovanovich, Inc. All rights reserved.

15. Please _____ those dishes.

16. _____ knew all my favorites.

17. The baby's _____ was a bright pink.

18. _____ that bill!

19. Podunk's basketball _____ has never won a game.

20. Every sentence _____ a verb.

Copyright © 1992 by Harcourt Brace Jovanovich, Inc. All rights reserved.

2

Multiple Subjects and Verbs

Some sentences have more than one subject. Others have more than one verb. Many sentences have more than one subject *and* more than one verb. The subjects in the following sentences have been labled with an "S" and the verbs with a "V."

<pre>
S   V   V
I washed and waxed my car.
</pre>

<pre>
      S   S   V
My brother and his wife adopted a baby girl.
</pre>

<pre>
      S   V   S   V
The President gave a speech, and then reporters asked him questions.
</pre>

<pre>
     S   V   S   V
Tim's checks often bounce because he never balances his checkbook.
</pre>

You can identify the pattern of a sentence by indicating how many subjects and verbs it has. Although in theory a sentence can have any number of subjects and verbs, these are the most common patterns:

S-V	one subject and one verb
S-V-V	one subject and two verbs
S-S-V	two subjects and one verb
S-V/S-V	two subjects and two verbs

Underline the subjects of the following sentences *once* and the verbs *twice*.

The bright light bothered my eyes.

The bank opens at ten and closes at four.

Grenada and Mongolia use Walt Disney cartoons on their postage stamps.

The election was important, but few people bothered to vote.

Any group of words that contains *at least one subject and one verb* is called a **clause.** A single sentence may have one clause, or more than one clause:

S-V	one clause	The teacher spoke to the class.
S-V-V	one clause	Tom listened and laughed.
S-S-V	one clause	Carlos and Lisa arrived.
S-V/S-V	two clauses	Pete left / when the bell rang.
S-V-V/S-V	two clauses	Ron waited and listened, / but we left.

Later in the book we will study the different types of clauses to understand how they determine punctuation. But for now the important thing is to learn to find *all* the subjects and verbs in each sentence.

Something to keep in mind when looking for multiple subjects and verbs is that the *length* of the sentence won't tell you whether the sentence has one clause, or several clauses. Look at these two sentences:

We leave if it rains. (How many clauses?)
The tired old football coach slowly climbed up the long ramp. (How many clauses?)

The first sentence is short, only five words, but it has two S-V patterns and, therefore, two clauses (*we leave* and *it rains*). The second sentence is more than twice as long, but it has only one clause (*coach . . . climbed*). So don't be fooled by the length of the sentence: some short sentences have multiple subjects and verbs, and some long sentences have only a single clause (S-V).

The sentences below are skeleton sentences. That is, they are stripped down to only subjects and verbs and connecting words. Go through them underlining the subjects *once* and the verbs *twice*.

Luanne waited and waited.

Albert and Earnestina met and kissed.

The boy and the girl and the woman talked.

When it rains, it pours.

It pours when it rains.

We left after it rained.

Juan and we left after the rain started.

Della and Marie and Connie cried because George died.

Because George died, Della and Connie and Marie cried.

If you go, I stay.

Wendell awoke and yawned and stretched.

Wendell yawned and stretched after he awoke.

After he awoke, Wendell stretched and yawned.

Rise and shine! (Did you remember to put *You* in front?)

The practice sentences below have multiple subjects and verbs, but they also include the other types of words you studied in Chapter One. Before you try them, review that chapter quickly to remind yourself about **adverbs** and **infinitives**, which are never part of the verb, and about **adjectives** and **possessives**, which are not part of the subject. Underline verbs *twice*, subjects *once*:

Bill and Irene like to dance slowly.

The old man and the old woman were very good dancers.

Tanya and the tall stranger danced and talked to each other.

Gary waited, but his old flame never arrived.

If the textbooks arrive, go and buy one.

Go and buy your Spanish textbook if it comes today.

Jill's book fell, and the tall boy retrieved it.

The very forgetful history professor forgot to remember his wedding anniversary.

The history professor's wife remembered but said nothing.

The professor's wife remembered, but she said nothing.

His wife remembered and reminded him, and they went out to eat.

This very long sentence's verb is not really an extremely large word.

EXERCISE 2A

Underline the subjects of the following sentences *once* and the verbs *twice*.
Remember not to include infinitives as part of the verb. To help you, the pattern of each sentence is indicated in parentheses.

1. Stress is an unavoidable part of life. (S-V)

2. Extreme or persistent stress sometimes causes physical illness or emotional problems. (S-V)

3. Sudden changes seem to trigger the worst stress. (S-V)

4. The loss of a loved one or a divorce or the loss of a job are examples of stressful changes. (S-S-S-V)

5. The digestive tract is particularly vulnerable to stress reactions. (S-V)

6. Upset stomachs, ulcers, and bowel disorders often occur at times of stress. (S-S-S-V)

7. Some women have menstrual disorders, and some men under stress become impotent. (S-V/S-V)

8. Many heart problems occur or become worse just after someone loses a job or separates from a wife or husband. (S-V-V/S-V-V)

9. Stress often triggers depression or severe anxiety. (S-V)

10. If you are in a stressful situation, you ought to try to reduce its effects on your body and on your emotions. (S-V/S-V)

Copyright © 1992 by Harcourt Brace Jovanovich, Inc. All rights reserved.

11. Think positively about future events under your control. (V)

12. Deal with your problems one at a time. (V)

13. Talk about your problems with your family and your friends. (V)

14. Listen to their opinions and advice, but avoid the role of complainer. (V/V)

15. Use exercise to relieve tension and to relax your body. (V)

16. If you get no regular exercise, begin a moderate exercise program. (S-V/V)

17. Nobody escapes the stress of life, but stress is manageable if we face it. (S-V/S-V/S-V)

Copyright © 1992 by Harcourt Brace Jovanovich, Inc. All rights reserved.

EXERCISE 2B

Underline the subjects of the following sentences *once* and the verbs *twice*. Some sentences have more than one subject, more than one verb, or both.

1. John Williams met Yvonne Lewis at a basketball game.

2. After they began to talk, they felt a strong mutual attraction.

3. When he asked her to meet him again, she agreed.

4. John and Yvonne had a good time on their first date.

5. They began to date regularly.

6. John looked forward to each date, but he noticed one peculiar fact.

7. Yvonne never wanted John to pick her up at her home.

8. She always arranged to meet him somewhere else.

9. Finally he asked Yvonne to explain.

10. She told him about her home life.

11. Her mother was dead, and her father was an alcoholic.

12. He sometimes became violent and once assaulted her previous boyfriend.

13. John told her to move away from home, but Yvonne refused because she had a ten-year-old sister.

14. She was afraid to leave the younger sister alone to deal with her father.

15. She also wanted to find a way to save her father.

Copyright © 1992 by Harcourt Brace Jovanovich, Inc. All rights reserved.

16. When John heard this, he surprised Yvonne by his words.

17. "Now I love you more than ever."

Copyright © 1992 by Harcourt Brace Jovanovich, Inc. All rights reserved.

EXERCISE 2C

The following sentences need more than one subject, more than one verb, or both. Put *one* noun, *one* subject pronoun, or *one* verb in each blank to complete each sentence.

1. The yellow _____ and the red _____ crashed.

2. The _____ sang beautifully, and the _____ applauded.

3. _____, _____, and _____ were old friends.

4. Jackie _____ the present and _____ it to her brother.

5. On Tuesday Roger _____ his license, and on Wednesday he _____ a car.

6. The bird _____ the worm and then _____ it.

7. When _____ got home, _____ helped her mom.

8. In 1989 Eileen _____ John, _____ her job, and _____ a baby.

9. _____ the old highway, and _____ at the third stop light.

Copyright © 1992 by Harcourt Brace Jovanovich, Inc. All rights reserved.

10. My sister _____ me a present, and my cousin

_____ my picture.

11. _____ the paint and _____ it slowly.

12. Len's _____ and Bev's _____ were

a good combination.

13. Albert _____ but _____.

14. First the sun _____; then the clouds _____.

15. _____ it slowly and _____ it care-

fully.

Copyright © 1992 by Harcourt Brace Jovanovich, Inc. All rights reserved.

3

Distinguishing Between Objects
of Prepositions and Subjects

One of the most common causes of errors in identifying the subject of a sentence is confusing it with a noun used as the object of a preposition. To avoid making this type of mistake, you first must learn to recognize prepositions and prepositional phrases.

Prepositions are the short words in our language that show the *position* or relationship between one word and another. For example, if you were trying to describe where a particular book was located, you might say:

The book is *on* the desk.
The book is *in* the drawer.
The book is *by* the table.
The book is *under* the notebook.
The book is *behind* him.

The italicized words are all prepositions. They show the position of the book in relation to the desk, the drawer, the table, the notebook, and him.

Here is a list of the most common prepositions. You do not have to memorize these words, but you must be able to recognize them as prepositions when you see them.

about	between	of
above	beyond	on
across	by	onto
after	concerning	out
against	down	over
along	during	through
amid	except	to
among	for	toward
around	from	under
at	in	up
before	inside	upon
behind	into	with
below	like	within
beneath	near	without
beside		

As you can see from the sentences describing the location of the book, prepositions are not used by themselves; they are always placed in front of a noun or pronoun. The noun or pronoun following the preposition is called the **object of the preposition.** The group of words containing the preposition and its object is called a **prepositional phrase.** Any words, such as adjectives or the words *a, an,* or *the,* which come between the preposition and its object are also part of the prepositional phrase. Read the following sentences, in which the prepositional phrases are italicized. Notice that each prepositional phrase begins with a preposition and ends with a noun or pronoun.

Julie studies *in the library.*
The children sat *beside their mother.*
Mike shares an apartment *with them.*
I drank two cups *of coffee.*

Some prepositional phrases may have more than one object.

The bank closes *on weekends and holidays.*
I like pizza *with pepperoni and anchovies.*

It is also possible to have two or more prepositional phrases in a row.

She sits *in the row behind me.*
The plane came *to a stop at the end of the runway.*

Circle the prepositional phrases in the following sentences. Some sentences may have more than one prepositional phrase.

We often walk along the beach.

The invitation to your party arrived in today's mail.

I drove around the parking lot for ten minutes.

The school closes during the months of July and August.

Construct sentences of your own containing prepositional phrases. Use the prepositions listed below. Make certain that each of your sentences contains at least one subject and one verb.

with: _____

_____

through: _____

_____

by: _____

_____

of: _____

_____

at: _____

_____

The words *before* and *after* may be used either as prepositions or as conjunctions (page 110). If the word is being used as a preposition, it will be followed by a noun or pronoun object. If the word is being used as a conjunction, it will be followed by both a subject and a verb.

As a Preposition	As a Conjunction

                                               S   V

The movie ended *before midnight.*   *Before* he does his homework, he eats a little snack.

                                                          S   V

He retired *after his seventieth birthday.*   We left the restaurant *after* we finished dinner.

What do prepositional phrases have to do with identifying subjects and verbs? The answer is simple.

Any word that is part of a prepositional phrase cannot be the subject or the verb of a sentence.

This rule works for two reasons:

1. Any noun or pronoun in a prepositional phrase must be the object of the preposition, and the object of a preposition cannot also be a subject.

2. Prepositional phrases never contain verbs.

To see how this rule can help you to identify subjects and verbs, read the following twenty-four-word sentence:

During my flight to Hawaii, the passenger in the seat beside me knocked a glass of orange juice from his tray onto my lap.

If you want to find the subject and verb of this sentence, you know that they will not be part of any of the sentence's prepositional phrases. So, cross out all the prepositional phrases in the sentence.

~~During my flight to Hawaii~~, the passenger ~~in the seat beside me~~ knocked a glass ~~of orange juice from his tray onto my~~ lap.

You now have only five words left out of the original twenty-four, and you know that the subject and verb must be within these five words. What are the subject and verb?

Read the following sentence, and cross out all of its prepositional phrases.

At night the lights from the oil refinery glow in the dark.

If you crossed out all the prepositional phrases, you should be left with only three words—*the lights glow.* Which word is the subject, and which is the verb?

Identify the subject and verb in the following sentence. Cross out the prepositional phrases first.

During the summer a group of students from local high schools came to

the university for special classes.

If you have identified all of the prepositional phrases, you should be left with only three words—*a group* and *came.* Which word is the subject, and which is the verb?

Now you can see another reason why it is important to be able to identify prepositional phrases. It might *seem* logical for the subject of the sentence to be *students.* However, since *of students* is a prepositional phrase, *students* cannot be the subject. Instead, the subject is *group.*

Underline the subjects of the following sentences *once* and the verbs *twice.* Remember to cross out the prepositional phrases first.

The celebration of the centennial of the Statue of Liberty occurred in 1986.

A family with five children lives next door to me.

All of the students finished the exam within an hour.

Two spaces in the parking lot are for people with physical disabilities.

The museum's collection of paintings includes works by famous Spanish

artists like Goya and El Greco.

At the beginning of the winter, the lack of snow hurt business at ski resorts.

The solution to the crossword puzzle appears at the back of the magazine,

but I never look at the answers.

When interest rates fall, the price of stocks will rise.

EXERCISE 3A

Underline the subjects of the following sentences *once* and the verbs *twice*. Some sentences may have more than one subject, more than one verb, or both. Remember to cross out the prepositional phrases first.

1. The newborn babies of monkeys join a social group.

2. At the time of birth, members of the group come to see the new baby.

3. The baby's eyes are open, and it already has fur.

4. It knows by instinct to cling to its mother as she uses her own hands and feet to get around in trees.

5. It clings to the underside of her body and goes everywhere with her.

6. The childhood of a monkey extends as long as three years.

7. At first it stays close to its mother, but then it begins to play with other young monkeys.

8. They chase each other, pull each other's tails, and play follow-the-leader.

9. These games of young monkeys teach them to live in a group and also to develop the physical skills for survival.

10. The fur of monkeys collects dirt, insects, and parasites.

11. All of the monkeys in a group like to groom each other's fur to keep it clean and to show affection for one another.

12. Young monkeys often groom the fur of their parents or other adults.

Copyright © 1992 by Harcourt Brace Jovanovich, Inc. All rights reserved.

13. If a young monkey is in danger, its mother or any nearby adult comes

to its aid.

14. From birth to death, monkeys need each other.

(This information was taken from *ZOOBOOKS* magazine, which features a scientifically accurate, thoroughly illustrated discussion of a different animal species each month.)

Copyright © 1992 by Harcourt Brace Jovanovich, Inc. All rights reserved.

EXERCISE 3B

Underline the subjects of the following sentences *once* and the verbs *twice*. Some sentences may have more than one subject, more than one verb, or both. Remember to cross out the prepositional phrases first.

1. Once upon a time, a large family lived on the tenth floor of a tall building in a big city.

2. The youngest daughter in the family called herself Tina because she hated her given name of Albertina.

3. All of Tina's older sisters had many boyfriends, but Tina was quiet and shy and afraid of boys at her high school.

4. When Tina looked from the window near her bed, she saw into an apartment across the street.

5. Several times a boy in that apartment waved at her, but she always ignored him.

6. One day she was home alone because she had the flu.

7. When she looked across at the boy's window, she saw a sign in his window.

8. "I am blue; I have the flu; you probably have it too."

9. Those words on his sign tickled her funny bone, and she forgot her shyness.

Copyright © 1992 by Harcourt Brace Jovanovich, Inc. All rights reserved.

10. She found a big piece of paper and a marker pen and put this sign in her window.

11. "I, too, have the flu, but I'm no longer blue, thanks to you."

12. For the rest of the day Tina and the boy across the street wrote messages back and forth through the silent air.

13. After breakfast the next day Tina's mother sent her off to school because she looked so happy, and Tina went gladly.

Copyright © 1992 by Harcourt Brace Jovanovich, Inc. All rights reserved.

EXERCISE 3C

Part One   A prepositional phrase adds more meaning to a sentence, but it also adds a noun or pronoun that may be mistaken for the subject. In each of the following sentences, underline the subject of the sentence *once* and the verb *twice*. Then *add* a prepositional phrase *between* the subject and verb. Does the subject change? The first sentence has been done as an example.

           to town
1. The <u>bus</u> ∧ <u><u>left</u></u> late.

2. The man laughed at the joke.

3. His awareness made her happy.

4. Those older actors got the most applause.

5. The questions were not very hard.

6. Bobbi's group won first prize.

7. The final hours seemed too short.

8. That textbook weighs about three pounds.

9. My sister received the present.

10. The oldest member made all-city honors.

Part Two   A preposition is always followed by its object, though it may not be the very next word. In each of the following sentences a preposition is missing its object. Put in a noun or a pronoun for the missing object. Then underline the subject of the sentence *once* and the verb *twice*. The first sentence has been done as an example.

           girls
11. <u>Three</u> of the ∧ <u><u>left</u></u> early.

Copyright © 1992 by Harcourt Brace Jovanovich, Inc. All rights reserved.

12. The view of the old made us feel good.

13. The captain of the team for this called the coin toss.

14. Her formula for was correct.

15. The smile on the small, red-headed, little boy's lit up the room.

16. The reason for the long unnecessary did not satisfy any of the customers.

17. He left because the safety light near the gray said "Danger."

18. Above the pleated, red silk she wore a black, sheer blouse.

19. Jan wants you to call if you find the part to her new, expensive.

20. Her answer to the puzzling made him see her in a new light.

Copyright © 1992 by Harcourt Brace Jovanovich, Inc. All rights reserved.

4

Main Verbs
and Helping Verbs

Verbs can be either **main verbs** or **helping** (also called **auxiliary**) **verbs.** Main verbs are the kind of verb you have already studied. Main verbs tell what action is being performed in a sentence. For example:

I *lost* my wallet.
The loud noise *frightened* us.

Helping verbs are used in combination with main verbs. They perform two major functions:

1. Helping verbs indicate shades of meaning that cannot be expressed by a main verb alone. Consider the differences in meaning in the following sentences, in which the helping verbs have been italicized.

   I *may* quit my job soon.
   I *must* quit my job soon.
   I *should* quit my job soon.
   I *can* quit my job soon.

As you can see, changing the helping verb changes the meaning of the entire sentence. These differences in meaning could not be expressed simply by using the main verb *quit* alone.

2. Helping verbs also show tense – the time at which the action of the verb takes place. Notice how changing the helping verb in the following sentences helps to change the tense of the main verb *watch*. (Both the helping and the main verbs have been italicized.)

The children *are watching* television now.
The children *will watch* television after dinner.
The children *have watched* television all evening.

Notice the position that helping verbs have in a sentence. They always *come before* the main verb, although sometimes another word, such as an adverb, may come between the helping verb and the main verb.

He *should buy* some life insurance.
He *should* probably *buy* some life insurance.
You *can lose* weight on this diet.
You *can* easily *lose* weight on this diet.

If a question contains a helping verb, the helping verb still *comes before* the main verb.

Will Congress *raise* taxes?
Can we *get* to the airport on time?
Do you *speak* Spanish?
Is the baby *sleeping* now?

The following words are helping verbs. *Memorize them.*

can, could
may, might, must
shall, should
will, would

The following words can be used either as helping verbs or as main verbs.

They are helping verbs if they are used in combination with a main verb. They are main verbs if they occur alone. *Memorize them.*

has, have, had	(forms of the verb *have*)
does, do, did, done	(forms of the verb *do*)
am, is, are, was, were, been	(forms of the verb *be*)

As Main Verbs	*As Helping Verbs*
I *have* two children.	I *have studied* French.
We *did* the assignment.	We *did* not *eat* breakfast.
She *is* here now.	She *is sleeping* now.

From now on, whenever you are asked to identify the verbs in a sentence, *include all the main verbs and all the helping verbs.* For example, in the sentence "We should review this lesson," the complete verb is "should review." In the sentence "He has lost his wallet," the verb is "has lost." Underline the complete verbs in the following sentences.

The team must win tomorrow's game.

Gail may marry Steve next year.

Children often do not like vegetables.

The class has already begun.

Some sentences may contain more than one helping verb.

one helping verb	The landlord *will increase* our rent.
two helping verbs	The plane *should be arriving* soon.
three helping verbs	The new highway *must have been completed* by now.

Underline the subjects of the following sentences *once* and the complete verbs *twice*.

The stores should be closing soon.

Did the sweater fit you?

Your friends must have been joking.

The children had borrowed books from the library.

Would you help me with this exercise?

I will go to the party if you can come with me.

Remember this rule:

The verbs in a sentence include all the main verbs plus all the helping verbs.

EXERCISE 4A

Underline the subjects of the following sentence *once* and the complete verbs *twice*. Some sentences may have more than one subject, more than one set of verbs, or both. Remember to cross out prepositional phrases first. Remember that *never* and *not* are adverbs and therefore are not part of the verb, even in a contraction like *cannot*.

1. Rattlesnakes hunt at night.

2. Because they cannot chew, they swallow their prey whole.

3. They lie in wait along the trail of some small animal like a rabbit or kangaroo rat.

4. A rattlesnake does not see well, but it does have an amazing organ to sense other animals.

5. This vomeronasal organ lies in the roof of the rattler's mouth.

6. After a rattlesnake flicks its tongue in the air, it retracts the tongue to the pits in the roof of its mouth.

7. The specialized organ there collects tiny molecules of air-borne information from the tongue of the rattler.

8. The snake's brain interprets the information and knows the type and size of the prey.

9. In one-quarter of a second the snake can strike, shoot poisonous venom into his prey, and pull back to a coiled position!

Copyright © 1992 by Harcourt Brace Jovanovich, Inc. All rights reserved.

10. The small animal will die quickly, and the rattler begins to slowly swallow his meal.

11. Rattlers do not normally hunt animals too large to swallow.

12. But many large animals like coyotes, eagles, wolves, and, of course, humans will eat rattlers, so in self defense they strike at any large animal in their territory.

13. Therefore, humans should be careful when they are walking in rattlesnake country.

Copyright © 1992 by Harcourt Brace Jovanovich, Inc. All rights reserved.

EXERCISE 4B

Underline the subjects of the following sentences *once* and the complete verbs *twice*. Some sentences may have more than one subject, more than one set of verbs, or both. Remember to cross out prepositional phrases first.

1. Although most birds shy away from cities, some birds seem to enjoy city life.

2. Pigeons have migrated from the dry areas of Mexico to the parks, lakes and ponds of most American cities.

3. One type of urban pigeon is the ringed turtle dove, but surprisingly it never leaves a small area of downtown Los Angeles.

4. The red-breasted robin loves the grassy lawns of schools, homes, and parks.

5. Although a robin with a cocked head seems to be listening for worms, the robin actually finds its favorite meal by its sense of sight.

6. The small house finches are very sociable birds, and they will gladly build a nest outside your apartment window or under the eaves of your roof.

7. If your house has a garden, you may find a mockingbird family in residence.

8. These talented birds imitate not only many other birds' songs but also the noises of cars, tractors, and sirens.

Copyright © 1992 by Harcourt Brace Jovanovich, Inc. All rights reserved.

9. The sparrow was introduced from Europe in New York city, and it spread from there in 1850 to California by 1870, and by 1990 from Alaska to the tip of South America.

10. In about a century and a half this single species of sparrow evolved into over twenty-six distinct sub-species.

11. The sparrow especially loves cities, and in some urban areas a species of local sparrow has evolved.

12. Some awful mistakes have been made by bringing birds into unfamiliar cities.

13. The first one hundred starlings were released in New York City in 1890 and by 1940 had spread throughout the U.S. as far as California.

14. Although starlings do feed on locusts and ground beetles, gigantic hordes of them now descend on fruit and vegetable crops and feedlots to cost farmers millions in damages each year.

15. Wildlife managers in Seattle, Washington, have regretted a decision to move some Canada geese to their city in the 1960s.

16. Now because the birds have multiplied and have dirtied the city's parks, city officials are exporting the big geese to hunting areas.

17. Sometimes birds love cities more than cities love birds.

(If you would like to know about the many different birds in your part of the country, get a copy of *The Audubon Society Field Guide* for your region.)

Copyright © 1992 by Harcourt Brace Jovanovich, Inc. All rights reserved.

EXERCISE 4C

Part One   Construct sentences of your own using the helping verbs listed below.

1. can: _____

_____

2. must: _____

_____

3. will: _____

_____

4. should: _____

_____

5. has: _____

_____

6. was: _____

_____

Part Two   Construct a sentence for each of the following patterns. Make certain that the order of the subjects and verbs in your sentences is the same as the order in the pattern. Use as many different helping and main verbs as possible.

S = subject   HV = helping verb   MV = main verb

7. S-MV:

8. S-MV-MV:

Copyright © 1992 by Harcourt Brace Jovanovich, Inc. All rights reserved.

9. S-HV-MV:

10. S-HV-HV-MV:

11. S-HV-HV-HV-MV:

12. HV-S-MV?: (Notice that this pattern produces a question, not a statement.)

Copyright © 1992 by Harcourt Brace Jovanovich, Inc. All rights reserved.

5

The Position of Verbals

In some languages the reader can always tell whether a word is a noun or verb or some other part of speech by just looking at the word. This is true of some words in English, but in most cases we have to see how a particular word fits into a sentence pattern before we can call it a "noun" or a "verb." Look at the word *trains* in these two sentences:

My brother trains horses for a living.
The trains rolled down the track.

Trains is a verb in the first sentence because it comes in a **verb position** in the sentence pattern. But in the second sentence *trains* is a noun because it comes in a **subject position.** The position of words is very important in English grammar. Saying that "John shot George" is very different from saying "George shot John." Some words in our language will shift into three or even four positions:

The people in that church *fast* during Lent.   (verb position)
Tony's *fast* took off five pounds.   (noun position)

The *fast* car had engine trouble.   (adjective position)
Eileen can run *fast*.   (adverb position)

This question of position in the sentence pattern is very important in seeing how one special group of words—**verbals**—plays a part in identifying subjects and verbs. **Verbals** are forms of verbs that, when placed in certain positions in the sentence pattern, will act like nouns or adjectives. Because verbals are closely related to verbs, you need to recognize them when you see them and not to confuse them with verbs. Verbals are **gerunds, participles,** or **infinitives.** Look at these sentences:

The man was *running*. (*running* in verb position = **main verb**)
Running was his hobby. (*running* in subject position = **gerund**)
The *running* man fell down. (*running* in adjective position = **participle**)
To run for a medal is his dream. (*To run* in subject position = **infinitive**)

Nouns (*car, pizza, Carla Smith*) and subject pronouns (*they, we, she*) are the most common subjects. But gerunds (*running, thinking, eating*) are also commonly used for subjects ("*Running* is her hobby"). Infinitives (*to run, to eat, to think*) are sometimes used as subjects also ("*To run* through the park is her favorite pastime"). To practice this, put first a noun, then a gerund, and then an infinitive in the three subject positions below:

_____ is not always easy. (Start with "The . . .")

_____ is not always easy.

_____ is not always easy.

Since gerunds and participles look alike because they both end in –*ing* ("The *rinsing* took twenty seconds" or "The *rinsing* solution came in a bottle"), the only way you can tell them apart is by their position in the sentence pattern. In these sentences, which are gerunds (subjects), and which are participles (modifiers of nouns)?

The washing machine is new.
The washing should take about five minutes.
Earning money gives a person self-respect.
Her earning power was reduced after her accident.

Notice that gerunds, like nouns, may be modified by adjectives and prepositional phrases:

The first *running* of the race was in July, 1988.
The sudden and fierce *rushing* of the wind blew over the shack.

Gerunds may also act like nouns in other ways. They may be objects or objects of prepositions. Again, the way you can tell the difference between the verb and the verbal is by position in the sentence pattern:

John is *running* the race again. (*running* as part of verb)
The thought of *running* again made him tired. (as object of preposition)
Sandra likes *running*. (as object of verb)

Notice that you would still have good sentences if you substituted nouns for the two gerunds.

The participles that we have looked at so far have all ended in *-ing*. These are called **present participles** because they come from verbs in the present tense ("The car is *rolling*"). When participles come from verbs in the past tense, they are called **past participles** ("The player was *injured*"). Past participles are also commonly used to modify subjects. Again you should notice the position of the participle before you decide whether it is being used as part of the verb or being used to modify a subject.

The player was *injured* badly.
The *injured* player left the game.
The students were *tired* by all the homework.
The *tired* students fell asleep.

Below is a group of sentences. Of course, they will all have verbs. But they will also include these **verbals**: gerunds as subjects, gerunds as objects of prepositions, gerunds as objects of verbs, infinitives as subjects, present participles as modifiers of nouns, and past participles as modifiers of nouns. First mark the *verbs* in the sentences. Then using the location of the verbal as your main clue, circle each *verbal* and label it as a "gerund" or "infinitive" or "participle." The first sentence has been done as an example:

gerund
              v
Her (winning) made us extremely happy.

The losing team left the court first.

The cost of painting surprised us.

To get high grades is not easy for everyone.

The paved road was shown in red.

The neglected road was paved by the city.

Her divorced parents are going to remarry.

Leaving this job would hurt my pocketbook.

The racing car flew off the track.

EXERCISE 5A

Underline the subjects of the following sentences *once* and the verbs *twice*. Remember that *gerunds*, as well as nouns and pronouns, can be subjects.

1. Smokers lose about 5½ minutes of life expectancy from each burning cigarette.

2. In other words, smoking one pack of cigarettes will cause a smoker to lose two hours of his or her life.

3. The mature smoker also faces such painful health problems as mouth and throat cancer, lung cancer, esophageal cancer, cancer of the bladder, emphysema, bronchitis, high blood pressure, hardening of the arteries, and heart attacks.

4. The non-smoking relatives and friends of smokers often wonder how smokers can continue such an irrational, life-destroying habit.

5. Smokers smoke because nicotine is extremely addicting for them.

6. Most smokers begin to smoke when they are careless teenagers.

7. They feel that they are going to be strong and healthy forever.

8. Many of their friends smoke, and smoking seems to be a sure symbol of maturity.

9. As they gradually go from puffing to inhaling, they never realize the signs of addiction.

Copyright © 1992 by Harcourt Brace Jovanovich, Inc. All rights reserved.

10. Four in five of practicing smokers want to quit smoking, but only twenty-five percent of them succeed in getting ''un-hooked.''

11. The withdrawal symptoms of nervousness, painful headaches, and extreme tension cause most smokers to fail no-smoking programs.

12. Nicotine is a strong drug, and its addicts cannot turn their backs on it without extreme pain and suffering.

Copyright © 1992 by Harcourt Brace Jovanovich, Inc. All rights reserved.

EXERCISE 5B

Underline the subjects of the following sentences *once* and the complete verbs *twice*. Remember that gerunds and infinitives, as well as nouns and pronouns, may be subjects. Also remember that participles, like adjectives, may modify nouns.

1. A barking dog seldom bites.

2. Every cloud has a silver lining.

3. Coming events cast their shadows before.

4. A bellowing cow soon forgets her calf.

5. Cowards die many times before their death.

6. A bleating sheep loses a bite.

7. A burnt child dreads the fire.

8. Everybody's business is nobody's business.

9. Marry in haste and repent at leisure.

10. Constant dripping will wear away a stone.

11. A fool and his money are soon parted.

12. The best doctors are Dr. Diet, Dr. Quiet, and Dr. Merryman.

13. A drowning man will clutch at a straw.

14. Faint heart never won fair maid.

15. When the going gets tough, the tough get going.

Copyright © 1992 by Harcourt Brace Jovanovich, Inc. All rights reserved.

16. The squeaking wheel gets the grease.

17. A fault confessed is half redressed.

18. Make haste slowly.

(What words are missing, though understood, in the next three sentences? What *kinds* of words are missing?)

19. Finders keepers, losers weepers.

20. Garbage in, garbage out.

21. Cold hands, warm heart.

Copyright © 1992 by Harcourt Brace Jovanovich, Inc. All rights reserved.

EXERCISE 5C

This exercise gives you practice in changing the location of verbals to give them a different job in the sentence.

Part One   For the sentences below, underline the subjects *once* and the verbs *twice*. Then below each sentence write a second sentence in which you change the *–ing* part of the verb into a **gerund** subject by moving it into the subject position. The second sentence does not have to have the same meaning as the first sentence. After you finish your new sentence, underline its subject and verb. The first pair has been done as an example.

1. The girl is running through the obstacle course.

Running through the obstacle course takes much energy.

2. John is teaching his sister.

_____

3. The coach is shouting at his players.

_____

4. Isaac has been working on his new car.

_____

5. Rachel will be kissing him goodbye soon.

_____

6. Dr. Williams is operating at 8:00 A.M.

_____

7. Our vacation will be beginning with a big party.

_____

Copyright © 1992 by Harcourt Brace Jovanovich, Inc. All rights reserved.

Part Two This part is about moving the location of the participle to change it from the main verb to a modifier of the subject. For the sentence below mark subjects and verbs as usual. Then make up a second sentence which uses the present or past participle of the verb as a participle modifying a subject. Circle your new modifier. *The second sentence does not have to have the same meaning as the first sentence.* Item number 8 has been done as an example.

8. The old <u>man</u> <u>was tired</u> from the work.
   The (tired) old man went to bed.

9. The house was painted by her brother.

10. The airplane is struggling through heavy fog.

11. Those items were collected after the fire.

12. The team was losing by a narrow margin.

13. The boat was drifting downstream rapidly.

Copyright © 1992 by Harcourt Brace Jovanovich, Inc. All rights reserved.

Subject-Verb Identification
Unit Review

Underline the subjects of the following sentences *once* and the complete verbs *twice*. Some sentences have more than one subject, more than one verb, or both.

Benedict Arnold is remembered for being one of America's greatest soldiers, and her greatest traitor.

Arnold was born in Connecticut in 1741. As a young man he, like George Washington, gained battle experience by fighting for the colonies in the French and Indian Wars. After these wars were over, he became a prosperous trader.

Early in the Revolutionary War against England, Arnold and Ethan Allen led joint forces to conquer Fort Ticonderoga. Then Arnold pushed on with his small army to destroy British ships and a fort at the north end of Lake Champlain.

In 1775 Arnold led an American expedition into Canada to take Quebec. After an incredibly difficult march, the force under Arnold was joined by another American army at the walls of the Canadian city. Beginning on December 31, the Americans besieged the city. Though Arnold was wounded, he continued the siege for several months but was finally driven back to Lake Champlain by the British. On the lake, Arnold built a small fleet of ships to keep the enemy from advancing south. Arnold's fleet was eventually defeated, but

Copyright © 1992 by Harcourt Brace Jovanovich, Inc. All rights reserved.

he had halted the enemy's march into the colonies. In 1776, despite General Washington's protests, the Congress promoted five generals of junior rank to be major generals over Arnold's head. Arnold remained bitter about this slight.

In the next few years, although Arnold continued his successful military career, several other events caused him to become even more bitter at the Revolutionary cause. He waged a brilliant campaign in New England and was promoted to major general, but he never regained his seniority in rank. In 1778 he married Peggy Shippen, a woman from a family still loyal to England. In 1779 Arnold was given command of West Point, a key fort on the Hudson River. He was given this important post even though he had just been cleared at a court martial for disputes with civilians and had been reprimanded by General Washington.

Arnold had already secretly begun a traitorous correpondence with the British. For a British commission and a sum of money, he had agreed to betray the American fort at West Point. Arnold's plot was discovered, but he escaped and began fighting for the British. He led two savage raids against Connecticut and Virginia before going into exile in England and Canada.

Wherever he lived, Arnold was scorned for his treachery. The term "a Benedict Arnold" lives on as a synonym for a traitor.

Copyright © 1992 by Harcourt Brace Jovanovich, Inc. All rights reserved.

*SUBJECT–VERB
AGREEMENT*

6

Recognizing Singular and Plural Subjects and Verbs

Errors in **subject–verb agreement** are among the most common grammatical mistakes. By applying the rules in this unit, you should be able to correct many of the errors in your own writing.

As you already know, a sentence must contain both a subject and a verb. Read the following two sentences. What is the grammatical difference between them?

The restaurant opens at noon.
The restaurants open at noon.

In the first sentence, the subject *restaurant* is singular. **Singular** means "one." There is only *one* restaurant in the first sentence. In the second sentence, the subject *restaurants* is plural. **Plural** means "two or more." There are at least two (and possibly more than two) restaurants in the second sentence.

Like the subject *restaurant*, the verb *opens* in the first sentence is singular. Verb forms ending in *s* are used with *singular* subjects, as in the sentence "The restaurant accepts credit cards.'' The verb *open* in the second sentence above is **plural.** This verb form (without a final *s*) is used with *plural* subjects, as in the sentence "The restaurants accept credit cards."

In other words, if the subject of a sentence is *singular*, the verb in the sentence must also be *singular*. If the subject of the sentence is *plural*, the verb must be *plural*. This matching of singular subjects with singular verbs and plural subjects with plural verbs is called **subject–verb agreement.**

In order to avoid making mistakes in subject–verb agreement, you must be able to recognize the difference between singular and plural subjects and verbs.

The subjects of sentences are usually nouns or pronouns. As you know, the plurals of nouns are usually formed by adding an *s* to singular forms.

Singular	*Plural*
envelope	envelopes
restaurant	restaurants

However, a few nouns (under 1 percent) have irregular plural forms.

Singular	*Plural*
man	men
child	children
knife	knives
thesis	theses
medium	media (as in the "mass media")

Those pronouns that can be used as subjects are also singular or plural, depending upon whether they refer to one or to more than one person or thing.

Singular	*Plural*
I	we
you	you
he, she, it	they

Notice that the pronoun *you* may be either singular or plural.

If nouns show number by adding *s* to the plural, what do verbs do to show whether they are singular or plural? A long time ago English verbs had many different endings for this purpose, but most of those endings have been dropped. Today most English verbs look the same whether the subject is singular or plural: "I see," "we see," "the boys see," "I jumped," "they jumped," "the frogs jumped," and so on. However, there is one place where English verbs have kept a special ending to show number. That special ending is also an *s*, and the only place it is added is the **present tense singular** with the subject pronouns *he, she, it,* and with any singular noun that could replace *it.* Look at these sentences in the present tense and notice when the *s* comes on the verb:

Singular	*Plural*
I see.	We see.
You see.	You see.
He see**s.**	They see.
She see**s.**	They see.
It see**s.**	They see.
The boy see**s.**	They see.
The girl see**s.**	They see.
The cat see**s.**	They see.
One nurse cares for him.	Three nurses care for him.

To sum up, although adding an *s* to most nouns (99 percent) makes them plural, some singular verbs also end with an *s.* An easy way to remember this difference is to memorize this rule:

Any verb ending in s is singular.

There are no exceptions to this rule. Therefore, it is not **good usage** in college writing to have a sentence in which a plural subject is matched with a verb ending in *s.* Effective writers are as aware of **usage** as they are of grammar.

Good usage means choosing different kinds of language for different situations, just as we choose different clothes for different situations. In **informal** situations, such as conversations with friends, it is common to choose informal usage. However, almost all of the writing you do for college is in **formal** situations, such as exams and essay assignments. The difference between formal and informal usage can be seen when we make subjects agree with their verbs. Because most conversation is very informal, you may have heard or have used many informal verb choices in your own conversations. Notice the differences in usage in these examples:

Informal	*Formal*
We was good friends.	We were good friends.
That don't sound right.	That doesn't sound right.
They was angry with the decision.	They were angry with the decision.

You want your college writing to be as effective as you can make it. In college you must choose **formal usage** in almost every situation—essays, reports, exams and so on. The exercises in our text are *always* designed for you to choose formal usage.

In order to avoid subject–verb agreement errors, there are some rules that you should keep in mind. (How you "keep rules in mind" is up to you. If you find that even after you study rules, you still cannot remember them, you should memorize the rules in this unit.)

Rule 1. A verb agrees with the subject, not with the complement. A **complement** is a word that refers to the same person or thing as the subject of the sentence. It follows a linking verb.

>   S   LV   C
> Our main *problem is* high prices.

In the sentence above, the subject is *problem*, which is singular. The subject is not *prices*. Rather, *prices* is the complement. Therefore, the linking verb takes the singular form *is* to agree with *problem*. If the sentence is reversed, it reads:

>   S   LV   C
> High *prices are* our main problem.

The subject is now the plural noun *prices*, and *problem* is the complement. The verb now takes the plural form *are*. Which are the correct verbs in the following sentences?

> The topic of conversation (was, were) the latest movies.
> Beans (is, are) the main ingredient in this recipe.

Rule 2. Do not mistakenly make your verb agree with a noun or pronoun in a prepositional phrase. (This is easy to do because many prepositional phrases come just before a verb.)

A *woman* with four children *lives* in that house.

In the sentence above, the subject is singular (*woman*). The prepositional phrase *with four children* has no effect on the verb, which remains singular (*lives*).

One of the colleges has a soccer team.

The singular verb *has* agrees with the singular subject *one*, not with the plural object of the preposition (*colleges*).

Which are the correct verbs in the following sentences?

The length of women's skirts (seems, seem) to change every year.
The cause of his many successes (are, is) obvious.

Rule 3. Be especially alert for subject–verb agreement when the sentence has **inverted word order** as in these three situations:

a) **questions**

Notice the location of the subject in these questions:

HV S MV
Do they like that class? (subject between helping and main verb)

V S
Is Reynaldo your best friend? (subject after main verb)

Interrogative words like *when, where,* and *how* come at the beginning of sentence patterns, but they are never subjects.

HV S MV
When *does* your *bus leave*? (subject between helping and main verb)

V S
Where *are* her *books*? (subject after verb)

HV S MV
How *did he make* the team? (subject between helping and main verb)

b) **sentence patterns beginning with *here* or *there***

Notice the location of the subject in these patterns:

There *are* fifty *states* in the United States. (subject after verb)
Here *is* your old chemistry *notebook*. (subject after verb)

The words *here* or *there* are never subjects.

c) **rare patterns in which the verb precedes the subject**

Occasionally a writer will, for emphasis, put a subject after its verb. Notice the location of the subject in these sentences:

Among his most valuable possessions *is* an antique *car*. (If the order of this sentence were reversed, it would read, "An antique *car is* among his most valuable possessions.")

In the middle of the wall *hang* two large *paintings*. ("Two large *paintings hang* in the middle of the wall.")

EXERCISE 6A

Circle the verb that correctly completes each sentence. Choose formal usage. Make certain that you have identified the correct subject of the sentence and that you have crossed out prepositional phrases. Remember that the word *salmon*, like the word *deer*, can be singular or plural.

1. Certain fish like salmon (live, lives) in the ocean but swim into freshwater rivers to breed and to spawn.

2. When rivers in highly industrialized countries become polluted, the salmon (quit, quits) visiting those rivers.

3. In Tokyo, schoolchildren from more than 100 elementary schools (is, are) trying to bring back the salmon to Tokyo's Nogawa River.

4. For many years the garbage and sewage of Tokyo (have, has) kept the salmon out of its river.

5. Now each year groups of schoolchildren (have, has) learned to breed, hatch, and release 100,000 small salmon into the Nogawa.

6. In 1979 a group of environmentalists in Tokyo began the Come Back Salmon Society, and they (have, has) enlisted the aid of the schoolchildren as part of their broader program to educate people about the rapid decay of Japan's environment.

7. The Japanese children (communicate, communicates) with their counterparts in other countries.

Copyright © 1992 by Harcourt Brace Jovanovich, Inc. All rights reserved.

8. Groups similar to the Japanese society (has, have) been at work on the Thames river in England and on the rivers of British Columbia in Canada.

9. In Washington state an Adopt-A-Stream program (involve, involves) about 20,000 people in the effort to improve the salmon habitat.

10. Over ninety schools and community groups (is, are) now helping to restore and restock Washington's streams.

11. Salmon (shows, show) particular sensitivity to polluted water.

12. If a watershed won't support a salmon run, then the area's humans (are, is) in danger too.

13. Clean streams for salmon (means, mean) a healthy environment for humans.

Copyright © 1992 by Harcourt Brace Jovanovich, Inc. All rights reserved.

EXERCISE 6B

Some of the sentences in this exercise contain subject–verb agreement errors. Others are correct as written. If the sentence contains a subject–verb agreement error, cross out the incorrect verb, and write the correct verb in its place. If the sentence is correct, write a *C* in the margin by the sentence number.

1. The restaurant open at 5:00 P.M.

2. The doors of the restaurant open at 11:30 A.M.

3. In the middle of the library stand a statue of an Egyptian goddess.

4. All of these stores accept credit cards.

5. Those old knives in the drawer are John's.

6. We was friends in the ninth grade.

7. Is Caroline your best friend?

8. That noise in the cylinders doesn't sound right.

9. A woman with three children live in that house.

10. Here are their old photograph.

11. Among the stolen items were his favorite jazz record.

12. How does the old man from the suburbs know his way around?

13. Her main complaint are the prices.

14. Do the sight of dead soldiers make you a pacifist?

15. There is over forty people in her psych class.

Copyright © 1992 by Harcourt Brace Jovanovich, Inc. All rights reserved.

16. When do the last one of the green buses leave?

17. The subject of his essay was the causes of the Vietnam War.

Copyright © 1992 by Harcourt Brace Jovanovich, Inc. All rights reserved.

EXERCISE 6C

In the following sentences change each plural subject to its singular form and each singular subject to its plural form. As you change the subject, change its verb to agree with it. The first sentence has been done as an example.

            sisters   like
1. My ~~sister~~ ~~likes~~ ice cream.

2. There is the solution to the puzzle.

3. The pilot in the cockpit is speaking.

4. How has your uncle been feeling?

5. The appetizers for the party were ready.

6. The fortunate side effect of the transaction was a new attitude.

7. The boat's sails reflect the sun.

8. His excuses for the mistake include a lack of time.

9. Among the cheerleaders were top gymnasts.

10. The coat with the vertical stripes makes him look taller.

11. The answers for that problem need some discussion.

12. Her hair-dos attract much attention.

13. There are no good responses to that question.

Copyright © 1992 by Harcourt Brace Jovanovich, Inc. All rights reserved.

14. The bystander near the accident on the freeway has given testimony.

15. Does your brother know?

16. On the wall hangs the team's plaque for the championship.

17. Her big problem has to do with her stubborness.

18. John's entry seems to have the lead.

Copyright © 1992 by Harcourt Brace Jovanovich, Inc. All rights reserved.

7

Indefinite Pronouns as Subjects

The subject pronouns we have been studying, like *she* or *it* or *they*, refer to specific, definite persons or things. This chapter is about another kind of pronoun, **indefinite pronouns,** which do not refer to a specific person or to definite things.

Rule 4. The following indefinite pronouns are singular and require singular verbs:

anybody, anyone, anything
each, each one
either, neither
everybody, everyone, everything
nobody, no one, nothing
somebody, someone, something

Everybody likes you.
Does everyone need a ticket?

Each of these jobs *pays* the minimum wage.
Either of those times *is* all right with me.

Notice that in the last two sentences, the verbs agree with the singular subjects *each* and *either*. The verbs are not affected by the plural nouns in the prepositional phrases *of these jobs* or *of those times*.

Rule 5. **Indefinite pronouns,** such as the words *some, half, most,* and *all*, may take either singular or plural verbs, depending upon their meaning in the context of the sentence. If these words tell **how much** of something is meant, the verb is singular; but if they tell **how many** of something is meant, the verb is plural.

Most of the milk *is* sour. (how much?)
These oranges look good, but *most* of them *are* sour. (how many?)
Some of the land *contains* gold. (how much?)
Some of the boxes *contain* money. (how many?)
All of the hospital *has* air conditioning. (how much?)
All of my children *have* the flu. (how many?)

(Do not confuse the words in this rule with the words *each, either*, and *neither* in Rule 4. These three words always require a singular verb.)

EXERCISE 7A

Circle the verb that correctly completes each sentence. Choose formal usage.

1. Some of the contestants (was, were) ready.

2. Someone with good work habits (is, are) going to get the job.

3. New problems with that machine (keeps, keep) cropping up.

4. The sale of lots in that subdivision (have, has) increased.

5. Most of John's customers (lives, live) nearby.

6. (Does, Do) neither of these desserts appeal to you?

7. Some of the cake at the dinner (was, were) left.

8. No one from her team (were, was) present.

9. (Has, Have) everyone received an invitation?

10. Near the old church (is, are) located her mother's grave.

11. Last week's performances (was, were) all sold out.

12. Here (is, are) seven good candidates for the position.

13. Half of the remaining tickets (is, are) reserved.

14. When (does, do) the first copies appear?

15. The expression on her features (has, have) fooled no one.

16. Everyone with a black eye (were, was) arrested.

Copyright © 1992 by Harcourt Brace Jovanovich, Inc. All rights reserved.

17. Through the center of the park (run, runs) many paths.

18. Where in the world (are, is) the maps for our trip?

19. The purpose of her visits (is, are) always money.

20. All of the building (are, is) considered fireproof.

Copyright © 1992 by Harcourt Brace Jovanovich, Inc. All rights reserved.

EXERCISE 7B

Some of the sentences in this exercise contain subject–verb agreement errors. Others are correct as written. If the sentence contains a subject–verb agreement error, cross out the incorrect verb and write the correct verb in its place. If the sentence is correct, write a *C* in the margin by the sentence number.

1. Some of Nancy's friends were there.

2. The faces of the old men with their tired look was sad.

3. Something in her eyes tells me to stay.

4. Her main interest at this time is his reasons for agreeing.

5. Most of those models has stereo.

6. The trouble with Tanya's photos is her giggling expression.

7. Does no one know the answer?

8. A house with so many windows are hard to heat.

9. Some of Terry's cake were too salty.

10. Nobody with a ticket was turned away.

11. How is any of the members supposed to know about the party?

12. Each of Betty's blouses are ironed.

13. Someone often take my place when I'm sick.

14. Most of the players arrive early.

15. One of the ingredients consist of a pre-mixed sauce.

Copyright © 1992 by Harcourt Brace Jovanovich, Inc. All rights reserved.

16. A few of the leaves from the tree has fallen.

17. His response to her repeated questions were three quick kisses.

18. The prices for each item on the list were shown in red.

19. There's five reasons not to go.

20. Something in my watchdogs's bark keeps the postman from delivering the mail.

Copyright © 1992 by Harcourt Brace Jovanovich, Inc. All rights reserved.

EXERCISE 7C

In the following sentences change all singular subjects to their plural form and all plural subjects to their singular form. If these changes affect subject–verb agreement, then change the verb to match the new subject. The first sentence has been done as an example.

        problems   were
1. The ~~problem~~ with the neighbors ~~was~~ their dogs.

2. The realtors' formula for success consists of three words: location, location, and location.

3. The man with the red mask, the sailor suit and the green shoes was the winner.

4. The outcome of the playoffs was three all-conference selections.

5. Women with ideas were encouraged to speak.

6. There is at this time some clue to the mysteries.

7. Her final triumph comes just in time.

8. The loot from the robberies includes bracelets, rings, brooches, and necklaces.

9. The lost doll was in the middle of the street.

10. Do most of the employees like their boss?

11. Their answer to the survey was quite shocking.

12. The buyer's reactions to her statement make no sense.

Copyright © 1992 by Harcourt Brace Jovanovich, Inc. All rights reserved.

13. The gang member is intelligent.

14. Why do the jurors insist on more information?

15. Over the doors hang the trophies from the league playoffs.

16. Has the half of the remaining pie been eaten?

17. Near the entrance sits a copy of "The Lovers" by Rodin.

18. Her children have an allergy.

19. Her gift is inexpensive.

Copyright © 1992 by Harcourt Brace Jovanovich, Inc. All rights reserved.

8

Subjects Understood
in a Special Sense

This chapter discusses as subjects several small groups of words that call for special attention in subject–verb agreement.

Rule 6. Some subjects, though **plural in form,** are **singular in meaning** and therefore require a singular verb. Such words include *news, mathematics, physics, economics, mumps,* and *measles.*

Mathematics is required for engineering majors.
Mumps makes it difficult to swallow.

Rule 7. A **unit of time, weight, measurement,** or **money** usually requires a singular verb because the entire amount is thought of as a single unit.

Two *hours was* not long enough for that test.
Fifty *dollars seems* a reasonable price for that jacket.
Four *ounces* of chocolate *is* needed for this recipe.

Rule 8. Collective nouns usually require singular verbs. A collective noun is a word that is singular in form but that refers to a group of people or things. Some common collective nouns are words such as *group, team, family, class, crowd,* and *committee.*

The *team practices* every afternoon.
The *crowd has been* very noisy.

Occasionally, a collective noun may be used with a plural verb if the writer wishes to show that the members of the group are acting as separate individuals rather than as a unified body. Notice the difference in meaning between the following pair of sentences:

The City Council has agreed to raise taxes. (In this sentence, *the City Council* is acting as a single, unified group.)

The City Council are arguing over a proposal to raise taxes. (In this sentence, *the City Council* is viewed as a collection of separate individuals who, because they are not in agreement, are not acting as a unified group.)

EXERCISE 8A

Circle the verb that correctly completes each sentence. Choose formal usage.

1. The news about the twins (make, makes) him very happy.

2. The Student Council (disagrees, disagree) with each other on this question.

3. Among her conquests (were, was) the captain of the football team.

4. Here (are, is) the answers for that chapter.

5. Fifty cents (doesn't, don't) buy a cup of coffee in that cafe.

6. Measles in a male (are, is) sometimes a serious disease.

7. How (have, has) the committee investigated her claim?

8. There (are, is) six goals for the coming year.

9. Three teaspoons of garlic powder (are, is) the secret to that recipe.

10. A crowd of three hundred (was, were) at the airport to meet the team.

11. The steward for the union members (insist, insists) on a meeting.

12. (Does, Do) your group expect to arrive on time?

13. Across the windows in front of the house (was, were) a row of jack-o-lanterns.

14. The management team never (have, has) won a softball game.

Copyright © 1992 by Harcourt Brace Jovanovich, Inc. All rights reserved.

15. Most of her advisors (were, was) women.

16. Physics (were, was) not his easiest course.

17. Anyone in the group (are, is) free to speak.

18. (Have, Has) the contest sponsors set a deadline?

Copyright © 1992 by Harcourt Brace Jovanovich, Inc. All rights reserved.

EXERCISE 8B

Some of the sentences in this exercise contain one or more subject–verb agreement errors. Others are correct as written. If the sentence contains a subject–verb agreement error, cross out the incorrect verb, and write the correct form in its place. If the sentence is correct, write *C* in the margin by the sentence number. This exercise covers rules from Lessons 6–8.

1. By the time a woman realizes she is pregnant, a series of remarkable changes have begun in her body.

2. Hormonal changes shut down her ovaries so that she ceases to ovulate each month.

3. Within the uterus, the embryo is already growing rapidly; through the fifth to twelfth weeks it grow from the size of a grain of rice to the size of a small potato.

4. After six weeks the embryo is called a fetus, and it now have a heart, a nervous system, eyes, and ears.

5. Many pregnant women shows little sign of their condition until their fifteenth week; but rapid changes continues inside the body.

6. Within the mother's uterus is the placenta; this special lining of the uterus during pregnancy is discarded after birth.

7. Extending from the placenta to the baby's abdomen are the umbilical cord with its fetal blood supply.

Copyright © 1992 by Harcourt Brace Jovanovich, Inc. All rights reserved.

8. Blood from the fetus flow back and forth through this cord carrying nourishment to the fetus and waste away from it.

9. Special cells (*villi*) on the placental wall is present to maximize the exchange of materials through the umbilical cord.

10. Near the end of the pregnancy the fetus usually drop down into the pelvic cavity and the baby's head points downward in preparation for birth.

11. Everything in the months of pregnancy have led to this moment.

Copyright © 1992 by Harcourt Brace Jovanovich, Inc. All rights reserved.

EXERCISE 8C

Some of the sentences in this exercise contain subject–verb agreement errors. Others are correct as written. If the sentence contains a subject–verb agreement error, cross out the incorrect verb, and write the correct form in its place. If the sentence is correct, write *C* in the margin by the sentence number. This exercise covers rules from Lessons 6–8.

1. Nineteen dollars was too much for that toy.

2. Cockroaches exists where many animals could not survive.

3. Where was your sister's child when the lights went out?

4. Her three days of illness uses up her sick leave.

5. The physics courses were her favorites.

6. Under this mountain goes two tunnels.

7. The causes of Aretha's success are hard work and talent.

8. None of that dessert were low in calories.

9. The selection board get together once a month.

10. Two gallons of gas in Europe cost as much as seven dollars.

11. Have his group of beginners been told about the scoring?

12. There are certainly no good reason to be worried.

13. No one in the group of tourists speak English.

14. Some of the cheeses were from Switzerland.

Copyright © 1992 by Harcourt Brace Jovanovich, Inc. All rights reserved.

15. Sometimes no news is good news.

16. The mice seems to be unafraid of Johnny's cat.

17. Does economics make any sense to you?

18. Her family leave on vacation next Tuesday.

Copyright © 1992 by Harcourt Brace Jovanovich, Inc. All rights reserved.

9

When Subjects Are
Joined by Conjunctions

Subjects joined by conjunctions require the special rules in this chapter.

Rule 9. Two subjects joined by the conjunction *and* are plural and require a plural verb.

Maine and *Idaho* both *grow* large amounts of potatoes.

Rule 10. When *each, every,* or *any* is used as an adjective in front of subjects, the subjects that are modified require a singular verb. (Writers have the most trouble with this rule when the sentence has two or more subjects joined by *and,* so this rule is an exception to Rule 9 above.)

Every car and motorcycle *needs* license plates.
Each cafe and deli *is inspected* by the Board of Health.

Notice that the adjectives *every* and *each* make the verbs in the sentences singular even though each sentence has more than one subject.

Rule 11. Two singular subjects joined by the conjunctions *or* or *nor* are singular and require a singular verb.

Soup or *salad is included* with your meal.
Neither the *supermarket* nor the *drugstore sells* nails.

Rule 12. If both a singular and a plural subject are joined by *or* or *nor*, the subject that is **closer** to the verb determines whether the verb is singular or plural.

Either *checks* or a credit *card is* acceptable at this hotel.
Either a credit *card* or *checks are* acceptable at this hotel.
Are travelers *checks* or a credit *card accepted* at this hotel?
Is a credit *card* or travelers *checks accepted* at this hotel?

(Note: in the final two sentences it is the *helping* verb that agrees.)

EXERCISE 9A

Circle the verb that correctly completes each sentence.

1. That image of her love (exists, exist) only in his imagination.

2. Neither Leroy nor Nathaniel (has, have) ever been to the city.

3. Any abrasive or chemical cleaner (damage, damages) the surface.

4. Carrots and turnips (were, was) his favorite vegetables.

5. Somebody usually (lose, loses) something on the bus.

6. (Does, Do) every coach and team member know the rules?

7. Her understanding of the relevant facts (impress, impresses) the jury.

8. Either a good tow or a strong hoist (were, was) necessary.

9. Someone without any prejudices (are, is) needed for the job.

10. Each forward and guard (are, is) taught specific play patterns.

11. Everyone at the fashion show (were, was) impressed by the styles.

12. The frame on the painting and its location (detract, detracts) from its value.

13. Pitzer and Johnson (is, are) considered the two best women players in the state.

14. Neither her headache nor her noisy baby (keep, keeps) Janet from doing her chores.

Copyright © 1992 by Harcourt Brace Jovanovich, Inc. All rights reserved.

15. Traffic lights and pedestrians (appear, appears) dimly out of the fog.

16. Either Ted or his sisters (is, are) available to babysit.

17. (Do, Does) Irene and her neighbors get along?

18. Where (has, have) most of the team been eating?

Copyright © 1992 by Harcourt Brace Jovanovich, Inc. All rights reserved.

EXERCISE 9B

Some of the sentences in this exercise contain subject–verb agreement errors. Others are correct as written. If the sentence contains a subject–verb agreement error, cross out the incorrect verb, and write the correct form in its place. If the sentence is correct, write *C* in the margin by the sentence number. This exercise covers rules from Lessons 6–9.

1. Occupational medicine study the links between occupation and disease.

2. Diseases of this type are most likely to be found in highly industrialized societies.

3. The most common of these diseases is respiratory-system disorders.

4. Dusty substances or certain chemicals in the workplace causes these disorders.

5. Dust diseases such as silicosis or asbestosis are typical of respiratory-system disease.

6. Among victims of this disorder is miners, stone masons, asbestos workers, and aluminum foundry workers.

7. Dockworkers or handlers in contact with animal products or pelts are in danger of the deadly disease of anthrax.

8. Some occupations are especially susceptible to eye diseases.

9. Loggers and metal grinders and polishers are known to suffer exceptionally high rates of eye injury from airborne particles of wood and metal.

Copyright © 1992 by Harcourt Brace Jovanovich, Inc. All rights reserved.

10. Raynaud's disease often affect handlers of vibrating machinery.

11. The jackhammers used to break up concrete pavement is probably the worst offender.

12. The result of this disease is loss of circulation in the hands and feet.

13. In certain occupations, many workers and sometimes a nearby employee is subject to extremely high levels of noise.

14. When these noise levels are sustained for very long, they gradually induce irreversible hearing loss.

15. There is seldom a job without some occupational risk.

16. Anyone working at a desk for many years are more likely to develop coronary artery disease.

17. Every employee and worker in any occupation is smart to take advantage of all the available safety precautions.

Copyright © 1992 by Harcourt Brace Jovanovich, Inc. All rights reserved.

EXERCISE 9C

Some of the sentences in this exercise contain subject–verb agreement errors. Others are correct as written. If a sentence contains a subject–verb agreement error, cross out the incorrect verb and write the correct verb in its place. If a sentence is correct, write a *C* in the margin by the sentence number. This exercise covers rules from Exercises 6–9.

1. Jack Williams and Sandra Lewis has been engaged for two weeks.

2. Here are the stories about the accident.

3. Neither the *Boomers* nor the *Bullets* is in contention for the championship.

4. Measles are now treated with large doses of gamma globulin.

5. Every bride and groom are required to take that blood test.

6. Neither Miller's hook shots nor Jone's defensive ability was enough to save the game.

7. There are in these circumstances no need to go to court.

8. The slices of lemon were floated on the punch.

9. The junior varsity team consist of freshmen and sophomores.

10. The teacher and her students share a mutual respect.

11. Have some of the assistant cooks arrived?

12. The new committee vote on every motion.

13. Under the bridge sails a large, blue-hulled sloop.

Copyright © 1992 by Harcourt Brace Jovanovich, Inc. All rights reserved.

14. Economics are required for all business administration majors.

15. Among her memories is a favorite recollection of summers on a farm.

16. How have the board members decided on the budget?

17. Either the rats or the mice has eaten those scraps.

18. Each man and woman in the audience feel the power of the speaker's words.

Copyright © 1992 by Harcourt Brace Jovanovich, Inc. All rights reserved.

Subject-Verb Agreement
Unit Review

Correct any subject–verb agreement errors that you find in the following essay by crossing out the incorrect verb and writing in the correct form. It may help you to underline all the subjects in the essay *once* and all the verbs *twice* before you try to identify errors in agreement.

Beautiful, healthy plants may be grown indoors if the indoor gardener are aware of their special needs. Like all container plants, indoor plants need porous soil, thorough watering, and mild, frequent doses of fertilizer. But indoor plants has certain additional requirements.

The container soil for an indoor plant must be entirely sterile. The confined root mass and low level of light for indoor plants encourages the growth of the harmful organisms in ordinary garden soil. These organisms kills even the healthiest house plant. You can buy a sterile soil medium, or you can sterilize your own soil. To do this, spread the soil in a shallow pan of no more than four inches and bake it for at least two hours at 180°. (This baking produce, briefly, a strong, unpleasant odor.)

The best water for indoor plants is rainwater. If none are available, and if your water system use softened water, get your water from an

Copyright © 1992 by Harcourt Brace Jovanovich, Inc. All rights reserved.

outside tap. If you must use softened water, give your plants a thorough leaching once a month. *Leaching* simply mean flushing the plant soil several times with fresh water.

Indoor plants need lots of good light but not the hot, direct sunlight through south and west windows. Either a northern or eastern exposure give indoor plants the best quality of light. Thin curtains are necessary for plants facing south and west windows. Flowering plants generally requires more light than non-flowering plants.

Indoor plants hate low humidity. They does best in humid rooms like bathrooms and kitchens, providing the light is adequate. If you really want to kill your house plant, put it near a hot-air register. Plants co-exists with heaters, if they're not too neighborly.

Anyone with the desire and a few dollars to spare are capable of having a lovely indoor garden. Treat indoor plants like other container plants, but also remember a few other basic points. Sterile soil, lots of soft light, rainwater, and moderate to high humidity is needed to make those philodendrons or that tiger lily look so good in your living room.

Copyright © 1992 by Harcourt Brace Jovanovich, Inc. All rights reserved.

IDENTIFYING AND PUNCTUATING THE MAIN TYPES OF SENTENCES

10

Compound Sentences

A **compound sentence,** a very common sentence pattern, contains *at least two subjects and two verbs,* usually arranged in an S-V/S-V pattern. For example:

Congress passed the bill, but the President vetoed it.
The television program received low ratings, so the network cancelled it.

In grammar, the term **compound** means "having two or more parts." Thus, the sentence "My *brother* and his *wife* are both engineers" has a **compound subject.** "The car *ran* out of gas and *stalled* in the intersection" has a **compound verb.**

A compound sentence can be divided into two parts, each of which can be a separate sentence by itself.

Congress passed the bill.
         +
The President vetoed it.

The television program received low ratings.

$$+$$

The network cancelled it.

Since a compound sentence can be divided into *two* separate sentences, each half of a compound sentence must contain at least one subject and one verb. Therefore, each half of a compound sentence is a **clause.** A clause is a group of words that contains both a subject and a verb. (In contrast, a group of words that does not contain both a subject and a verb is called a **phrase,** as in a prepositional phrase.) A clause that can stand alone as a complete sentence is called an **independent clause.** Since each clause in a compound sentence can stand alone as a complete sentence, each clause must be independent. In other words:

A compound sentence consists of at least two independent clauses joined together to form a single sentence.

There are two ways to join independent clauses in order to form a compound sentence. The most frequently used method is to put a conjunction between the clauses. A **conjunction** is a word that joins words or groups of words. In grammar, the word *coordinate* means "of equal importance." Therefore, the conjunctions that are used in compound sentences are called **coordinating conjunctions** because they join two groups of words that are of equal grammatical importance. (They are both independent clauses.) The following coordinating conjunctions are used to join the clauses of compound sentences:

and
but
for (when it means *because*)
or
so
yet

You should *memorize* these coordinating conjunctions because later you will have to be able to distinguish between them and the connecting words that are used to form other kinds of sentences.

In the following sentences, underline the subjects of the compound sentences *once* and the verbs *twice*, and circle the coordinating conjunction that joins the clauses. Notice that a comma **precedes** the coordinating conjunction.

The critics disliked the movie, but the public loved it.

The jury found the defendant guilty, and the judge sentenced him to five years in prison.

You can't park in this space, for it is reserved for the handicapped.

I never smoke, nor does my husband. (Notice that when *nor* is used to join two independent clauses, the pattern becomes S-V/V-S: *He has* no children, nor *has she*.)

You should move your car, or you may get a ticket.

The college needed more money, so it raised its tuition fee.

I have a good driving record, yet my car insurance costs went up.

Construct compound sentences of your own, using the coordinating conjunctions listed below to join your clauses. Underline the subject of each clause *once* and the verb *twice*. (You may construct a clause that has more than one subject and/or more than one verb, but each clause must have *at least* one subject and one verb.)

_____, and _____

_____, but _____

_____, for _____

_____, or _____

The second way to join the clauses in a compound sentence is to use a semicolon (;) *in place of both the comma and the coordinating conjunction.* For example:

I appreciate your suggestions; they have really helped me.
The test is tomorrow; we should study tonight.

Compound sentences constructed with semicolons occur less frequently than compound sentences constructed with coordinating conjunctions because some type of connecting word is usually needed to show the relationship between the clauses. For example, without a coordinating conjunction the logical relationship between the two clauses in the following sentence might be confusing.

Democracy requires a lot of patience; it is the fairest system.

If, however, you replace the semicolon with a coordinating conjunction, the relationship between the clauses becomes clear.

Democracy requires a lot of patience, *but* it is the fairest system.

· It is all right to use the semicolon by itself between the clauses of a compound sentence, but do so only when the relationship between the clauses is clear without a connecting word.

Construct two compound sentences of your own, using semicolons to join the clauses. Underline the subjects *once* and the verbs *twice*. Make certain that each clause has at least one subject and one verb.

_____; _____

_____; _____

Another common way to show the relationship between the clauses of a compound sentence is to use a **conjunctive adverb,** like *however,* in the second clause. Notice that a semicolon is required between the clauses.

Democracy requires a lot of patience; *however,* it is the fairest system.

Conjunctive adverbs are especially frequent in formal language where the precise relationship between ideas is the goal. Here are most frequently used conjunctive adverbs:

also	incidentally	nonetheless
anyway	indeed	otherwise
besides	instead	still
consequently	likewise	then
finally	meanwhile	therefore
furthermore	moreover	thus
hence	nevertheless	
however	next	

A conjunctive adverb gets its double name from the fact that it does two things at once: it connects, like other **conjunctions,** and it modifies, like other **adverbs.** Because it is adverbial, it can be located in many places in its own clause. And because it can move around in the second clause and does not always come *exactly between* the two clauses (like coordinating conjunctions), it does not necessarily act as a signal to readers that they are coming to the second half of a compound sentence. For these reasons, the strong signal of a semicolon marks the end of the first clause.

> Lou wanted a challenging career; *therefore,* he became a brain surgeon.
> Lou wanted a challenging career; he, *therefore,* became a brain surgeon.
> Lou wanted a challenging career; he became a brain surgeon, *therefore.*
> Maya is a good friend; we don't, *however,* always get along.

(Notice that the conjunctive adverb is always "set off" with a comma, or two commas, in its own clause.) Construct three compound sentences of your own that use *conjunctive adverbs.* Try putting the conjunctive adverb in several different places in the second clause.

1. _____

_____

2. _____

_____

3. _____

_____

(Did you remember to "set off" the conjunctive adverb with one or two commas?)

As you can see from the sentences that you have constructed in this lesson, the following punctuation rules apply to compound sentences:

1. If the clauses in a compound sentence are joined by a coordinating conjunction, place a comma before (to the left of) the conjunction.

This sentence is compound, and it contains a comma.

You may have learned that it is not necessary to use commas in short compound sentences (for example, "He's a Scorpio and I'm a Libra"). Although this is true, not everyone agrees on how short a "short" compound sentence is, so if you are in doubt, it is safer to use a comma. All the sentences in the exercises for this unit will be "long" compound sentences and should have a comma before the conjunction.

2. Although a compound sentence may contain more than one coordinating conjunction, the comma is placed before the conjunction that joins the clauses.

Alice *and* Ray are married, *and* they are also best friends.

3. If the clauses in a compound sentence are *not* joined by a coordinating conjunction, place a semicolon between the clauses.

Chemistry is my major; I try my hardest to make *A*'s in it.
John knew the law; however, he did not always obey it.
The candidate covered up his record; he, consequently, was able to fool the voters.

The following sentence patterns do *not* require commas because they are **simple** (meaning that they contain only one clause) rather than compound.

S-V-V	I went to the bank and deposited my check. (no comma)
S-S-V	Physics and chemistry are required for a nursing major. (no comma)
S-S-V-V	The workers and the factory owners agreed to a contract and prevented a strike. (no comma)

To review, the two patterns for punctuating a compound sentence are:

clause + comma + coordinating conjunction + clause
The boxer was badly injured, so the referee stopped the fight.

clause + semicolon + clause
I'm not sleeping; I'm just resting my eyelids.
I'm tired; however, I cannot sleep.

EXERCISE 10A

Make each of the following independent clauses a compound sentence by adding an appropriate coordinating conjunction and a second independent clause. Try to use as many different conjunctions in this exercise as possible. Remember to place a comma before the coordinating conjunction.

1. My aunt is a widow _____

   _____

2. Larry and Lori are engaged _____

   _____

3. This restaurant will seat ninety customers _____

   _____

4. The coach insists on strict discipline _____

   _____

Write compound sentences of your own, using the coordinating conjunctions listed below. Remember to place a comma before the coordinating conjunction that divides the clauses, and make certain that each of your clauses contains at least one subject and one verb.

5. but: _____

   _____

6. so: _____

   _____

Copyright © 1992 by Harcourt Brace Jovanovich, Inc. All rights reserved.

7. and: _____

_____

8. or: _____

_____

9. nor: _____

_____

10. for: _____

_____

11. yet: _____

_____

Construct four compound sentences punctuated with semicolons. In two of them use a conjunctive adverb in the second clause.

12. _____

_____

13. _____

_____

14. _____

_____

15. _____

_____

Copyright © 1992 by Harcourt Brace Jovanovich, Inc. All rights reserved.

EXERCISE 10B

Add commas and semicolons to the following sentences wherever they are needed. If a sentence needs no additional punctuation (in other words, if the sentence is simple rather than compound), label it *C* for *correct*.

1. The confusing arrangement of letters on most typewriter and computer keyboards is no accident; the inventor needed to deceive his customers.

2. Christopher Sholes developed the first commercially produced typewriter in 1873 he arranged its keyboard in alphabetical order.

3. Sholes' typewriter was superior to its competitors in most ways however it had one serious drawback.

4. It typed flawlessly at low speeds but at high speeds the little striking levers jammed.

5. Sholes asked his brother-in-law for help in solving the problem and the brother-in-law came up with a solution.

6. He arranged the keys according to frequency of use thus the top line of keys began as Q W E R T Y.

7. The new arrangement of keys worked but Sholes decided on a deception to justify his odd keyboard.

8. He described his keyboard as a "scientifically-tested keyboard" for the fastest possible typing.

Copyright © 1992 by Harcourt Brace Jovanovich, Inc. All rights reserved.

9. Sholes' keyboard was not at all efficient instead it forces the typist's fingers to travel much farther than necessary for most letters.

10. No one caught on to Sholes' deception most of his competitors even copied the Q W E R T Y arrangement.

11. Some of Sholes' competitors tried to market alternative keyboards but those companies failed.

12. We are stuck today with Sholes' inefficient keyboard arrangement from the 19th century however several much more efficient arrangements for keyboards have been designed to be easier to teach and faster to type.

13. The preceding material comes from *The Book of Lies* by M. Hirsh Goldberg it was published in 1990.

14. The *Book of Lies* details several hundred schemes, scams, fakes, and frauds from Biblical times to the present.

15. All the lies and scams in Goldberg's book are alike in one respect; they changed the course of history and continue to affect our daily lives today.

Copyright © 1992 by Harcourt Brace Jovanovich, Inc. All rights reserved.

EXERCISE 10C

All the sentence patterns listed below have multiple subjects, multiple verbs, or both. But some patterns are for *simple* sentences, and other patterns are for *compound* sentences. Write a sentence for each pattern. If a sentence is *compound*, apply one of the two punctuation rules for compound sentences.

1. S-V-V: _____

_____

_____

2. S-V-S-V: _____

_____

_____

3. S-V-V-S-V: _____

_____

_____

4. S-S-V: _____

_____

_____

5. S-V-V-V: _____

_____

_____

6. S-V-S-S-V: _____

_____

_____

Copyright © 1992 by Harcourt Brace Jovanovich, Inc. All rights reserved.

7. S-S-V-V: _____

_____

_____

8. S-S-V-S-V: _____

_____

_____

Combine each pair of *simple* sentences into one *compound* sentence. Try different methods for each sentence.

9. False friends desert in times of trouble. True friends prove themselves.

_____

_____

10. Some men express a deep hatred for women in private. They are often extremely polite to women in public.

_____

_____

11. The past is gone forever. We can choose to remember it as history.

_____

_____

12. Pascal tells us to "gamble" on the existence of God. It's a win-win situation.

_____

_____

13. *Progress* is difficult to define. One person's labor-saving power lawn mower is another person's Sunday-morning nuisance.

_____

_____

Copyright © 1992 by Harcourt Brace Jovanovich, Inc. All rights reserved.

11

Complex Sentences

There are two kinds of clauses, independent and dependent. As you have seen in Lesson 8, **independent clauses** can stand alone as complete sentences. For example:

John speaks three languages.
Astronomers have discovered a new galaxy.

A **dependent clause,** however, *cannot* stand alone as a complete sentence. Instead, it must be attached to, or *depend* upon, an *independent* clause in order to form a grammatically complete sentence and to express a complete idea. Notice that the following dependent clauses are *not* complete sentences.

If it rains tomorrow . . .
Whenever I write an essay . . .
After she won the state lottery . . .

These clauses seem incomplete because they are actually only *part* of a sentence. Using the first of the following sentences as a model, change each dependent clause into a complete sentence by adding an appropriate *independent* clause.

If it rains tomorrow, _____ *I won't wash my car.* _____

Whenever I write an essay _____

_____

After she won the state lottery _____

_____

You have now constructed two complex sentences. A **complex sentence** contains both independent and dependent clauses. (In contrast, a **compound sentence** contains only *independent* clauses.)

Every dependent clause begins with a subordinating conjunction. A **conjunction** joins words or groups of words. The conjunctions that begin dependent clauses are called **subordinating conjunctions** because the word *subordinate* means "of lesser importance." Grammatically speaking, a dependent clause is "less important" than an independent clause because it cannot stand alone as a complete sentence. In contrast, the conjunctions that you used in the previous lesson to form compound sentences are called **coordinating conjunctions** because *coordinate* means "of equal importance." Since both of the clauses in a compound sentence are independent, both clauses are "of equal importance."

The type of dependent clause that you will be studying in this lesson is called an **adverb clause** because, like another adverb, an adverb clause describes a verb (or sometimes an adjective or an adverb). It is the same kind of clause that you worked with in Lesson 2. The subordinating conjunctions used to begin adverb clauses describe verbs by telling *how, when, where, why* or *under what conditions* the action occurs.

> *how:* as if, as though
> *when:* after, as, as soon as, before, until, when, whenever, while
> *where:* where, wherever
> *why:* because, in order that, since, so that
> *under what conditions:* although, as long as, even though, if, though, unless

Read the following sentences. A slanted line indicates the point at which each sentence divides into two separate clauses. Underline the subject of each clause *once* and the verb *twice*. Circle the subordinating conjunction.

Because Paul lifts weights,/he is very muscular.

When you finish the test,/you may leave.

I usually read the paper/while I eat breakfast.

Now in each sentence examine the clause that contains the circled subordinating conjunction.

The clause that contains the subordinating conjunction is the dependent clause.

Notice that in a complex sentence, the dependent clause may be either the first or the second clause in the sentence.

If you like spy stories, you should read the novels of John Le Carré.
We won't get married *until we graduate*.

In most cases, the adverb clauses in a complex sentence are *reversible*. That is, the sentence has the same basic meaning no matter which clause comes first. For example.

Whenever I buy groceries, I try to use coupons.
I try to use coupons *whenever I buy groceries*.

or

Before the game began, the crowd sang the national anthem.
The crowd sang the national anthem *before the game began*.

However, the order of the clauses in a complex sentence does affect the punctuation of the sentence.

1. If the **dependent** clause is the first clause in the sentence, it is followed by a comma.

If I have enough money, I'll buy a new car.

2. If the **independent** clause is the first clause in the sentence, no comma is needed.

I'll buy a new car *if I have enough money*.

Punctuate the following complex sentences. First circle the subordinating conjunction in each sentence, and draw a slanted line between the clauses.

I'll return your books after I eat lunch.

If you keep your old clothes long enough they'll eventually come back into fashion.

Although I can read Spanish I can't speak it well.

Unless you have a good credit rating it is difficult to borrow money from a bank.

EXERCISE 11A

Complete each of the following complex sentences by adding an appropriate adverb clause (one that makes sense in the sentence). Add commas where they are necessary.

1. Marie left early for work although _____

_____

2. Whenever _____

_____

we call my Uncle Fred.

3. Before _____

_____

the boat crashed into the rocks.

4. Johnny was taken to the hospital because _____

_____

_____

5. All nations may some day live together in peace if _____

_____

6. Teresa will make a good president because _____

_____

Copyright © 1992 by Harcourt Brace Jovanovich, Inc. All rights reserved.

Construct complex sentences of your own, using the following subordinating conjunctions to form your adverb clauses. Add commas where they are necessary.

7. _____ wherever

_____

8. _____ so that

_____

9. _____ even though

_____

10. _____ since

_____

11. Because _____

_____

Convert each pair of simple sentences below into a single complex sentence by adding a *subordinating conjunction* to the front of one of the simple sentences. Think carefully: Will either of the simple sentences make a better independent clause? Many correct combinations are possible.

12. Marla is an expert hairdresser. She will make you look terrific.

_____

_____

13. I lent Jack ninety dollars once. He won't lend me any money.

_____

_____

Copyright © 1992 by Harcourt Brace Jovanovich, Inc. All rights reserved.

14. Irene has always voted the Democratic ticket. She is campaigning for a Republican candidate.

_____

_____

15. Most of our body's functions are performed automatically. On our conscious choices we are free to act.

_____

_____

16. No woman has ever been a U.S. president. Americans tend to stereotype women as "followers."

_____

_____

Copyright © 1992 by Harcourt Brace Jovanovich, Inc. All rights reserved.

EXERCISE 11B

Determine which sentences below are *complex* by underlining their *dependent* clauses. Then add commas to the sentences if they are necessary. If a sentence needs no additional punctuation, label it *C* for *correct*.

1. Many people do not like bats because these animals have the reputation of being evil or dangerous.

2. Since we fear such diseases as rabies from bats each year people spend millions of dollars to exterminate bats.

3. In all the records of the U.S. Health Service, there are only ten cases of people getting rabies from bats.

4. Household pets are much more likely than bats to cause rabies.

5. Because they look like rats with wings people fear bats and associate them with Halloween monsters.

6. Bats, however, are extremely beneficial to humans, and we should be protecting not destroying them.

7. Since bats are nature's way of controlling moths, mosquitoes, and other insects we very much need bats for our well-being.

8. The 20 million bats flying nightly out of Bracken Cave, Texas, are a typical example of the value of bats.

9. Each night this bat colony consumes 250,000 pounds of mosquitoes and insects, and, unlike pesticides, the bats do no harm to the environment.

Copyright © 1992 by Harcourt Brace Jovanovich, Inc. All rights reserved.

10. Half of all tropical fruits like bananas, papayas, and mangoes become pollinated because a bat has visited the blossom.

11. Bats provide this service free.

12. You may not care for their looks, but, honestly, bats are your good friends.

Copyright © 1992 by Harcourt Brace Jovanovich, Inc. All rights reserved.

EXERCISE 11C

Part One For each different *type* of subordinating conjunction, write a complex sentence with an adverb clause. The adverb clause may come at the beginning or at the end of the sentence.

1. a subordinating conjunction that shows *why* the action occurs:

_____

_____

2. a subordinating conjunction that shows *where* the action occurs:

_____

_____

3. a subordinating conjunction that shows *how* the action occurs:

_____

_____

4. a subordinating conjunction that shows *when* the action occurs:

_____

_____

5. a subordinating conjunction that shows *under what conditions* the action occurs:

_____

_____

Copyright © 1992 by Harcourt Brace Jovanovich, Inc. All rights reserved.

Part Two Combine each pair of sentences below into a single complex sentence by joining them with a subordinating conjunction. Think carefully: Which sentence will make the best dependent clause and which conjunction will make a meaningful connection? Punctuate your new complex sentence.

6. Marshall studied hard. He took the test.

_____

_____

7. Elmer started the fight. He was angry with John.

_____

_____

8. Her bus arrives at 11:30. We will say goodbye.

_____

_____

9. Harry can open this lock. We can get the door open.

_____

_____

Copyright © 1992 by Harcourt Brace Jovanovich, Inc. All rights reserved.

12

Compound–Complex Sentences, Comma Splices, and Run-On Sentences

When a compound sentence includes a dependent clause, that type of sentence is called a **compound-complex** sentence. The dependent clause may be in either main clause.

> I will go *if you do*, but I want to stay here.
>
> or
>
> Engine-powered vehicles have replaced the horse and ox, but some people would like to go back to the "good old days" *because cars, trucks, trains, and planes make pollution and noise.*

In compound–complex sentences we can see the operation of all the punctuation rules that we have studied up to now. In the examples below of compound–complex sentences, notice how important it is to recognize the three different types of joining words: coordinating conjunctions, subordinating conjunctions, and conjunctive adverbs. (See chart inside front cover of textbook.)

The main clauses of a compound–complex sentence may be joined with a comma and a coordinating conjunction.

You should plant the garden quickly, **or** you should wait **until** the storm has blown over.

The main clauses of a compound–complex sentence may be joined with only a semicolon.

World War I was supposed to end all wars; World War II came **after** only twenty years had passed.

When a conjunctive adverb is used in the second main clause, a semicolon is needed between the main clauses.

It is very difficult to make laws about controversial issues like abortion; **however,** a law may be created **because** the public demands some resolution to the issue.

When a dependent adverbial clause comes *after* its main clause, it is *not* set off with a comma.

I like most desserts**, but** I don't eat strawberries **because** I'm allergic to them.
or
I don't eat strawberries **because** I'm allergic to them**, but** I do like most desserts.

When a dependent adverbial clause comes in front of its main clause, it *is* set off with a comma.

I like most desserts**, but because** I'm allergic to strawberries**,** I don't eat them.
or
Because I'm allergic to strawberries, I don't eat them**, but** I do like most desserts.

Run-Ons and Comma Splices

With any type of sentence, two of the most serious punctuation errors are **run-on sentences** and **comma splices.** These errors send the wrong signals to the reader, causing the reader to misread your words or confuse your meaning. (Some of the errors you corrected in the exercises for Lessons 10 and 11 were comma splices and run-ons, although they were not identified as such.)

A **run-on sentence** occurs when one sentence is run into the following sentence with no punctuation.

We respect Ann she works hard.

A **comma splice** occurs when a comma alone is used between independent clauses.

We respect Ann, she works hard.

Comma splices and run-on sentences may be corrected in several different ways. The two clauses that we looked at above may be punctuated correctly as two simple sentences.

We respect Ann. She works hard.

But you should consider other equally correct possibilities which may express a slightly different emphasis or a slightly different meaning.

We respect Ann; she works hard. (compound)
We respect Ann, for she works hard. (compound)
Ann works hard; therefore, we respect her. (compound)
We respect Ann because she works hard. (complex)

Below are some comma splices and run-ons for you to correct. Correct each one two different ways. Use a variety of punctuation and/or connecting words.

He hates computers his Mom loves them.

1. _____

2. _____

I don't like tunnels, they scare me.

1. _____

2. _____

We saw a flock of geese, there were at least a dozen.

1. _____

_____

2. _____

_____

Though all sharks have common traits, they come in many different sizes and shapes each species is adapted to a particular prey and a particular hunting pattern.

1. _____

_____

_____

2. _____

_____

_____

I am enjoying my psychology class it makes me think about the reasons for my behavior.

1. _____

_____

2. _____

_____

Comma splices and run-ons usually occur in definite patterns for different writers. For example, many writers often make these errors when a clause begins with a subject pronoun referring to a noun in the previous clause (as in the final sentence you corrected above). To find out if you have a definite pattern in the way that you make these errors, keep a list of your comma splices and run-ons. After you have collected half a dozen or more, go over them with your teacher. If you can discover a pattern, you will find it easier to keep from making these punctuation errors.

EXERCISE 12A

Part One All of the sentences below are compound–complex. Study each sentence carefully. Circle the subordinating conjunction and underline its dependent clause. (Which *independent* clause does it belong to?) Punctuate the whole sentence as a compound sentence. Then, if necessary, set off the dependent clause with a comma. If a sentence needs no additional punctuation, label it *C* for *correct*.

1. When Leila calls Mitchell he runs away quickly he thinks he's being funny.

2. Marie blushed for her smile gave her away even though she tried to hide it.

3. The ignition was off however the engine continued to run because it was so hot.

4. If she continues to set sales records she will be the new sales manager all of the employees would like that.

5. The boat slowed after the wind died yet we stayed ahead of the older boats.

6. Although her makeup was smudged no one noticed and she kept her composure.

7. The expedition began in a rainstorm no one cared because they were anxious to get started.

8. Although Leila is in kindergarten she can do many first-grade skills and she is strong like her dad.

Copyright © 1992 by Harcourt Brace Jovanovich, Inc. All rights reserved.

9. Leila's new baby sister is called Meaghan Marie because her mother likes that name and so does Leila.

10. They live next to a big, big woods when they look out their window, they see deer and wild turkeys.

11. She laughed after the baby smiled and the others laughed too.

Part Two Compose four compound-complex sentences and punctuate them carefully.

12. _____

_____

_____

_____

13. _____

_____

_____

_____

14. _____

_____

_____

_____

15. _____

_____

_____

_____

Copyright © 1992 by Harcourt Brace Jovanovich, Inc. All rights reserved.

EXERCISE 12B

The essay below includes simple, compound, complex, and compound–complex sentences, but they are not always punctuated correctly. The errors are comma splices and run-on sentences. Correct all the errors.

It's a tradition for the girls in our family to be cheerleaders because my great-grandmother was in the first group of cheerleaders at our high school in 1930 since then my grandmother, my mother, and my older sisters have led cheers and presided at pep rallies for good old Hoover High, naturally, I was expected to follow in their footsteps.

Yesterday we had cheerleading tryouts, it was my chance to win my pompons. When I got up late, I told my mother about my sore throat, and she said, "The show must go on" so I went to the tryouts.

We were supposed to wear shorts or skirts to show off our great legs consequently I wore slacks. Coach Waller made me get my gray shorts from my gym locker, and I wore them inside out and backwards, the coach ignored me none of my schemes were working, I was getting close to winning a spot as a cheerleader.

Copyright © 1992 by Harcourt Brace Jovanovich, Inc. All rights reserved.

At the end of the tryouts we were supposed to form a giant pyramid I was the key person since I was at the top center standing on Dickie Pratt's shoulders. At the crucial moment I looked down and loudly said, "Why, Dickie! You're getting bald!" He was so mad! He twisted to shout something to me the whole pyramid collapsed in a tangle of arms and legs!

"The Hoover High cheerleading squad doesn't need nitwits!" Those were Ms. Waller's words when she sent me home, what a disgrace I am to my family! Maybe they will all quit talking to me would you like to have some used practice pompons?

Copyright © 1992 by Harcourt Brace Jovanovich, Inc. All rights reserved.

EXERCISE 12C

Below are several groups of simple sentences. Combine each group into a single compound–complex sentence by using the various ways for connecting clauses that we've studied in the past three lessons. Word your new sentence so that it makes sense and reads smoothly. (Several combinations are possible. You might want to try each sentence first on a piece of scratch paper.) The first sentence combination has been done as an example.

1. Rex did not pass the qualifying test for deep-sea diving.
   He will not become a certified diver.
   He is very disappointed.

   Because Rex did not pass the qualifying test for deep-sea diving, he will not become a certified diver; he is very disappointed.

2. Phillip is very smart.
   He never studies.
   He makes low grades.

   _____

   _____

   _____

3. The environment belongs to all.
   No one person can preserve it.
   One world disaster will destroy it.

   _____

   _____

   _____

Copyright © 1992 by Harcourt Brace Jovanovich, Inc. All rights reserved.

4. Exercise is cheap.
It's good for you.
Most people hate it.

_____

_____

_____

5. A home facing south has advantages.
The sun can come in during winter.
The sun can be blocked in summer.

_____

_____

_____

6. Many countries have abandoned communism.
They seek new social orders.
Chaos is almost certain.

_____

_____

_____

7. Women use all their brain at once.
Men tend to use one side at a time.
Their brains seem to work differently.

_____

_____

_____

Copyright © 1992 by Harcourt Brace Jovanovich, Inc. All rights reserved.

13

Correcting Fragments

The basic unit of expression in written English is the sentence. As you already know, *a sentence must contain at least one independent clause.*

If you take a group of words that is *not* a complete sentence and punctuate it as though it were a complete sentence, you have created a **sentence fragment.** In other words, you have written only a piece — a fragment — of a sentence rather than a complete sentence.

As you can see. Wrong punctuation. May be confusing.

Since semicolons and periods are usually interchangeable, fragments may also be created by misusing semicolons.

As you can see; wrong punctuation may be confusing.

If you look carefully at the two groups of words, you see that they should form a single, complex sentence which needs, at most, a comma.

As you can see, wrong punctuation may be confusing.

Although fragments occur frequently in speech and occasionally in informal writing, they are generally not acceptable in classroom writing and should be avoided in formal writing situations.

There are two types of fragments: **dependent clauses** and **phrases.**

As you have already learned (Lesson 11), a dependent clause cannot stand alone as a complete sentence. It must be attached to an independent clause in order to form a complex sentence.

Therefore, any dependent clause that is separated from its main clause by a period or semicolon is a fragment.

Below are several examples of this type of fragment.

When we exercise vigorously. We inhale more oxygen.
When we exercise vigorously; we inhale more oxygen.
We inhale more oxygen. When we exercise vigorously.
We inhale more oxygen; when we exercise vigorously.

Eliminate the dependent-clause fragments in the following paragraph by punctuating them correctly.

Textbooks for most classes may be purchased; before the class meets.

However, some professors do not want their students to purchase any texts.

Until the class has met for at least one session. These professors may use

the first class session to check each student's eligibility for that course. If

the student is not eligible; he or she will not be allowed to remain in the

course, and the student won't be the owner of an unwanted textbook. Most

students like this policy. Because the bookstore will not refund the full pur-

chase price. When an unused book is returned.

Are you remembering to punctuate each dependent clause according to its location? As you learned in Lesson 11, if the *dependent* clause is the first clause in a sentence, it should be followed by a comma. If the *independent* clause is the first clause in a sentence, no comma is needed.

The second type of fragment is the phrase. Since a **phrase** is defined as a group of words that does *not* contain both a subject and a verb, a phrase obviously cannot be a complete sentence. **All phrases are fragments.** Study the following types of fragments, and notice the way each phrase has been changed from a fragment into a complete sentence.

FRAGMENT – NO SUBJECT	Didn't finish the book.
SENTENCE	*John* didn't finish the book.
FRAGMENT – NO VERB	The cheerleaders on the field.
SENTENCE	The cheerleaders *are* on the field.
FRAGMENT – INCOMPLETE VERB (*-ing* form)	The cat watching the dog.
SENTENCE	The cat *was watching* the dog.
	(An *-ing* main verb must be preceded by a helping verb)
	or
	The cat watch*es* the dog.
	(Change the *-ing* form of the verb)
FRAGMENT – INCOMPLETE VERB (past participle)	The picture painted by Diana.
SENTENCE	The picture *was painted* by Diana.
	(To be a main verb, a past participle must be preceded by a helping verb. For an explanation and a list of past participles, see Lesson 26.)
FRAGMENT – INFINITIVE	To do the assignment correctly.
SENTENCE	*He wants* to do the assignment correctly.
FRAGMENT – PARTICIPLE	Watching Maria smile.
SENTENCE	*I like* watching Maria smile.

The following groups of words are fragments because they lack either a subject or a verb or because they have an incomplete verb. Rewrite each fragment so that it becomes a complete sentence.

To eliminate the funny noise in the motor.

Returning your phone call.

The film damaged by exposure to light.

Mailed your package for you.

The most expensive item on the menu.

The lineman accidentally tackled by the safety.

The candidates appearing in a debate.

When you are writing a composition, be careful not to separate a phrase from the rest of the sentence to which it belongs.

INCORRECT I've lost a small boy. Wearing red pants.
CORRECT I've lost a small boy wearing red pants.
INCORRECT Smiling from her victory; she took the prize.
CORRECT Smiling from her victory, she took the prize.

Rewrite the following items so that any fragmentary phrases are correctly joined with the sentences to which they belong.

The voters were angry. They signed a petition. Asking for a reduction in

property taxes.

My appointment was for late afternoon. Hoping to avoid heavy traffic; I

left my office at 3:00.

Lulled by the motion of the car. The child fell asleep in her car-seat.

To summarize: **phrases** are sentence fragments because they do not contain both a subject and a complete verb. (In other words, they are not clauses.) **Dependent clauses** are fragments because they are not *independent* clauses. This is simply another way of stating the most basic rule of sentence construction:

Every sentence must contain at least one independent clause.

EXERCISE 13A

In the essay below, some phrases and dependent clauses have been separated by periods or semicolons from the independent clauses to which they belong. Locate these *fragments* and correct them by attaching each to the correct independent clause. In some cases you should replace the period or semicolon with a comma, but in other cases no punctuation is required. You may need to change some capital letters to lower case letters.

If there are some very large black birds in your neighborhood. You may think of them as *crows*. These large birds, however, are probably *ravens*. Most people confuse *crows* and *ravens*. Because they are cousins from the same bird family. Called the *corvids*. And because they are very similar in appearance. Ravens, however, are more interesting birds than their cousins, the common crows.

The raven is called *corvus corax* by scientists; it differs physically from its crow cousin. The raven may weigh four times as much as a crow; the raven's wingspan may extend as much as four feet. A crow's wing has a blunt tip. Not pointed like a raven's wing. The two birds may also be differentiated by their tails. Because a crow has a squarish tail, but a raven's tail is shaped liked a wedge.

One of the most interesting things about ravens is the extent of their geographical and ecological range. Most bird species limit

Copyright © 1992 by Harcourt Brace Jovanovich, Inc. All rights reserved.

themselves to a relatively small area and a particular climate. Ravens, however, are found. Throughout every part of the earth. From above the Arctic Circle all the way south to the Andes Mountains. They live in every type of climate. From frozen Arctic ice floes to dense coniferous and deciduous forests. They live in the hot deserts of America and Africa. And at the fringes of many cities.

Most interesting of all is the raven's personality and behavior. Ravens live up to their beautiful, glossy black, irridescent plumage. They are the acrobats of the bird world. They love to dive and roll out of the sky or to speed through trees and swerve suddenly before obstacles. They are also the brains of the bird world. With their huge variety of birdcalls, they seem to speak back and forth incessantly. Like a group of chattering humans. Recent studies reveal extremely high levels of teamwork; among ravens in locating and sharing food. A raven community will fan out early in the day over a 1600-square-mile area for a day's hunting. When one of them finds food, he will signal "Food! Food!" to the rest of the flock.

Ravens have a bad image in some cultures. Because they scavenge dead bodies. But many cultures revere the raven as the most special of all birds.

Copyright © 1992 by Harcourt Brace Jovanovich, Inc. All rights reserved.

EXERCISE 13B

Each of the paragraphs below contains *comma splices, run-on sentences,* and *fragments.* Correct these errors using the methods you have learned from this lesson and the previous lesson.

Our sense of time changes with age and circumstance, small children live in the present they have little sense of the past or future. To small children, "yesterday" and "last week" mean about the same thing. They do not plan for the future; because it is not happening now.

The child's initiation into the adult's world of clocks and calendars begins with school, school separates the year into months. And into school times and weekends and vacation times. The child must be at school at a certain hour and minute. "School will begin at 8:15 A.M." Every room in the school has a clock. Because classes must be coordinated into a schedule. The children soon learn to anticipate recesses, lunch hours, and the time to go home.

School conditions children to prepare them for the adult world of time clocks, production schedules and deadlines, meetings must be attended monthly and quarterly reports become due. The time

Copyright © 1992 by Harcourt Brace Jovanovich, Inc. All rights reserved.

habits learned in school may make the difference between failure or success in the world of adult work employers don't want tardy employees or coffee-break cheaters in the workplace.

The modern, time-conscious person often has trouble enjoying a vacation. Away from the usual routine, the clock does not matter, no one is waiting for him or her to finish something. The sun rises at its own pace no one sets the alarm. The time-bound worker is suddenly free. "I could lie in bed all day!" "I could dance all night." "I could drift across the sky with the moon." "I am a small child again, I don't even know what time it is!"

Copyright © 1992 by Harcourt Brace Jovanovich, Inc. All rights reserved.

EXERCISE 13C

Show that you understand what a *comma splice* is by writing three of them. After you write each comma splice, correct it in the space provided. Use a different method to correct each one.

1. _____

_____

correction: _____

_____

2. _____

_____

correction: _____

_____

3. _____

_____

correction: _____

_____

Show that you understand what a *run-on sentence* is by writing three of them. After you write each run-on, correct it in the space provided. Use a different method to correct each one.

1. _____

_____

correction: _____

_____

Copyright © 1992 by Harcourt Brace Jovanovich, Inc. All rights reserved.

2. _____

_____

correction: _____

_____

3. _____

_____

correction: _____

_____

Show that you understand what *fragments* are by writing three different kinds of fragments. After you write each fragment, correct it in the space provided.

1. _____

_____

correction: _____

_____

2. _____

_____

correction: _____

_____

3. _____

_____

correction: _____

_____

Copyright © 1992 by Harcourt Brace Jovanovich, Inc. All rights reserved.

Correcting Comma Splices, Run-On Sentences and Fragments
Unit Review

Correct any comma splices, run-on sentences, or fragments in the following paragraphs.

If you have "perfect pitch," you are quite an unusual person, only about one person in two thousand has perfect pitch. What exactly is it? Perfect pitch is a cluster of abilities, these abilities allow a person to identify and remember any musical note without reference to any other note. If a person with perfect pitch hears any one key on a piano; he or she can not only identify the note but can also state if the piano was exactly "in tune."

For a long time perfect pitch has been considered a learned ability. Music teachers and music schools require special courses and special exercises to teach students to recognize the pitch of sample notes, many never master the skill.

Dr. Joseph Profita is a psychiatrist and amateur musician. He believes perfect pitch is a completely inherited trait; and has developed a test to prove it. Most other researchers in the field agree with him, they think he is on the right track. People with perfect pitch usually become aware of it. When they are children. They may have

Copyright © 1992 by Harcourt Brace Jovanovich, Inc. All rights reserved.

had no training in music whatsoever yet they identify notes effortlessly and immediately. We now know this fact. If a parent has perfect pitch. His or her son or daughter has a fifty percent chance of inheriting the trait.

Perfect pitch is not a requirement to be a great composer or even a great performer. Neither Willie Nelson nor Vladimir Horowitz has perfect pitch. Nor do many of history's great composers. But almost all musicians do have excellent "relative pitch." They may not be able to identify any particular note, but when they are told the name of that note they can connect it to other, related notes.

(The material in this review is condensed from a January, 1991, *New York Times* wire-service article by Sandra Blakeslee.)

Copyright © 1992 by Harcourt Brace Jovanovich, Inc. All rights reserved.

UNIT FOUR

PUNCTUATION THAT "SETS OFF" OR SEPARATES

14

Parenthetical Expressions

When speaking, people often interrupt their sentences with expressions such as *by the way, after all,* or *as a matter of fact.* These expressions are not really part of the main idea of the sentence; instead, they are interrupting—or **parenthetical**—expressions which speakers use to fill in the pauses while they are thinking of what to say next. In speech, people indicate that these parenthetical expressions are not part of the main idea of the sentence by pausing and dropping their voices before and after the expression. In writing, the same pauses are indicated with commas.

You have already learned that commas may be used to separate the clauses in compound and complex sentences. Another major function of the comma is to "set off" interrupting, or **parenthetical expressions** from the rest of the sentence in which they occur.

Read the following sentences aloud, and notice how the commas around the italicized parenthetical expressions correspond to the pauses you make in speech.

Well, the bus is late again.
This morning, *in fact,* it is almost twenty minutes late.
I'm going to be late for work, *I'm afraid.*

The rule for punctuating parenthetical expressions is very simple:

A parenthetical expression must be completely set off from the rest of the sentence by commas.

This means that if the parenthetical expression occurs at the *beginning* of the sentence, it is *followed* by a comma. For example:

On the whole, married men live longer than single men.

If the parenthetical expression is at the *end* of the sentence, it is *preceded* by a comma.

The capital of Michigan is Lansing, isn't it?

If the parenthetical expression is in the *middle* of the sentence, it is both *preceded* and *followed* by a comma.

Coal and diamonds, for example, both contain carbon.

There are many parenthetical expressions. Some of the most frequently used ones are listed below.

after all
as a matter of fact
at any rate
etc. (an abbreviation of the Latin words *et cetera*, meaning "and other
    things")
for example
for instance
furthermore
however
in fact
nevertheless
of course
on the other hand
on the whole
therefore
well (at the beginning of a sentence)
yes and *no* (at the beginning of a sentence)

Expressions such as the following are often parenthetical if they occur in a position *other than* at the beginning of a sentence.

does it
doesn't it
I believe
I suppose
I hope
I think
is it
isn't it
that is
you know

For example:

Today is payday, isn't it?
Eggs, you know, are high in cholesterol.

Continual repetition of the parenthetical expression *you know* should be avoided in both speech and writing. If you are speaking clearly and your listener is paying attention, he knows what you are saying and does not have to be constantly reminded of the fact. Besides, you know, continually repeating *you know* can be irritating to your listener; and, you know, it doesn't really accomplish anything.

Study the following points carefully.

1. Some of the above words and phrases can be either parenthetical or not parenthetical, depending upon how they are used in a sentence. **If an expression is parenthetical, it can be removed from the sentence, and the remaining words will still be a complete sentence.**

PARENTHETICAL   Congress, *after all*, represents the people.
NOT PARENTHETICAL   She was tired *after all* her work.
PARENTHETICAL   Ms. Walker's prose is better than her poetry, *I think*.
NOT PARENTHETICAL   Often *I think* about my childhood friends.

2. Since the abbreviation *etc.* is parenthetical, it must be *preceded* and *followed* by a comma if it occurs in the middle of a sentence.

Shirts, ties, shaving lotion, *etc.*, are typical Father's Day gifts.

The final comma after *etc.* indicates that *etc.* is parenthetical. Notice that this comma serves a different function from the commas that separate the items in the series.

3. **Conjunctive adverbs,** like *however* and *nevertheless*, are considered parenthetical and are set off in the clause in which they occur. They should be punctuated in simple sentences as follows:

   I don't like him. *However,* he is a good man to work for.

                              or

   I don't like him. He is, *however,* a good man to work for.

In the second clause of a compound sentence, **conjunctive adverbs** should be punctuated as follows:

   He is a good friend; *however,* we often disagree.
   She didn't study much; *nevertheless,* she received a *B.*

(Conjunctive adverbs have been discussed earlier in Unit Four. For a complete list of them see the inside front cover.)

4. People's names and titles are also set off by commas **if you are speaking directly to them** in a sentence. This type of construction is called **direct address.** The punctuation of direct address is the same as that used for parenthetical expressions.

   Ladies and gentlemen of the jury, have you reached a verdict?
   Mrs. Castro, will you speak to our club?

Notice that names and titles are set off by commas only when the person is being *directly addressed* in the sentence. Otherwise, no commas are needed.

   The package is for Donald. (no comma)
   Donald, did you get the package? (comma for direct address)

EXERCISE 14A

Part One   Add commas to the following sentences wherever they are necessary. If a sentence needs no additional punctuation, label it *C* for *correct*. The sentences in this section of the exercise deal only with the punctuation of parenthetical expressions.

1. The dictionary meaning of a word is called its *denotation.*

2. But words have other meanings not found in the dictionary don't they?

3. For example we could choose to call someone an ''officer of the law'' or to call that person a ''cop.''

4. *Officer of the law* has a respectful flavor; on the other hand the term *cop* has a flavor of disrespect.

5. These flavors that cling to words are in fact an essential part of their meanings; we call these flavors the *connotations* of words.

Part Two   Add commas and semicolons to the following sentences wherever they are necessary. If a sentence needs no additional punctuation, label it *C* for *correct*. This section covers the punctuation of compound and complex sentences as well as parenthetical expressions and direct address.

6. English is a language rich in *synonyms* that is English has many groups of words with similar dictionary meanings or *denotations.*

7. All of the terms in this group for example have the same denotation: *officer of the law, lawman, policeman, cop, fuzz,* and *pig.*

Copyright © 1992 by Harcourt Brace Jovanovich, Inc. All rights reserved.

8. However as you read through that group of terms from *officer of the law* to *pig* you feel an increasing flavor of disrespect, don't you?

9. In other words, each of those terms has a different connotation some are favorable and others quite unfavorable.

10. Connotation reveals the writer's attitude toward his subject and as a result shapes the audience's attitude to the subject at the same time.

11. Effective propagandists and advertisers are of course masters of *connotative* meaning because to be successful they must shape the attitudes of their audience.

12. We've all been shaped I suppose by the connotations of various words; that may be good or bad.

13. Words are power send them and receive them carefully.

Copyright © 1992 by Harcourt Brace Jovanovich, Inc. All rights reserved.

EXERCISE 14B

Add commas and semicolons to the following sentences wherever they are necessary. If a sentence needs no additional punctuation, label it *C* for *correct*. This exercise covers the punctuation of compound and complex sentences and parenthetical expressions.

Old people have special medical problems. For example their joints stiffen with age, their muscles shrink, and their circulation slows. For many old people the greatest fear is a loss of mental power. A major cause of this loss may be Alzheimer's disease.

This disease is hard to diagnose because its symptoms resemble the symptoms of several other disorders common to aging when a person shows a noticeable deterioration of memory or reasoning power, it may be due to Alzheimer's or it may be the result of a brain tumor, a glandular disorder, or a series of small strokes. The most certain sign of Alzheimer's disease is a progressive alteration of brain cells however this alteration is usually not detected until a post-mortem autopsy. Therefore many cases of Alzheimer's have gone undetected unless the patient has been quite young that is in the thirties, forties, or fifties. People with these symptoms after the age

Copyright © 1992 by Harcourt Brace Jovanovich, Inc. All rights reserved.

of sixty are usually considered "just old" and may get no special medical treatment.

Alzheimer's may be a cruel disease, depriving its victims of normal mental powers and emotional responses while their bodies remain relatively young and healthy. The disease is especially hard on close friends and relatives because they of course must stand by while the victim gradually becomes a mental and emotional vegetable. Alzheimer support groups developed in recent years have alleviated but cannot eliminate this tragic consequence of Alzheimer's.

Current medical research may improve the treatment for Alzheimer's and perhaps discover a cure for this dread disease. In fact researchers have discovered certain hormones that seem to arrest the degeneration of the victim's brain cells. And other researchers in genetic engineering may soon positively identify the genetic origin of Alzheimer's disease. It would be a miracle wouldn't it to see this curse lifted from our future?

Copyright © 1992 by Harcourt Brace Jovanovich, Inc. All rights reserved.

EXERCISE 14C

Add commas and semicolons to the following letter wherever they are necessary. This exercise covers the punctuation of compound and complex sentences and parenthetical expressions.

Mr. Dean Smith

All-Safe Insurance Company

Dear Mr. Smith:

I'm writing this letter to accompany my accident report because our accident last week with our brand-new motor home was too complicated to explain on your short form.

It all started with Lula's insistence that we buy a motor home with a picture window and commode at the rear. (You know what a *commode* is that's just a fancy word for a toilet.) Lula said, "When I'm sitting on the commode I want to look out the window and see where I've been."

On November 1, we started for Florida. Lula was driving, and I decided to use the commode. I was half way through the sports section when all of a sudden Lula slams on the brakes. She sees

Copyright © 1992 by Harcourt Brace Jovanovich, Inc. All rights reserved.

these two dogs, a Doberman and a pit bull, running right in front of our new RV. Of course I'm facing backwards therefore my head bashes into the wall. Then Lula hits the gas pedal and I flop against the EMERGENCY door and consequently I fly right out the back of the RV. Fortunately I was able to hang on to the door however my feet were dragging because my pants and shorts were hanging around my ankles. Something about this situation seemed to upset those two dogs because they made a beeline for my behind. For some reason Lula began to slow down therefore all I could do was kick off those pants and start running. When I passed Lula and she looked out and saw those two dogs just about to take chunks from my rear end she of course swerved right at them. Well that was a mistake because that's when she crashed into the pet-store window. This did however distract the dogs. They didn't know whether to chase all the loose cats or go after the chimpanzee. As you might guess, that's when the aquarium went through our windshield. Lula wasn't hurt too bad, it did stun her a bit but perhaps that was good because it seems to have erased all her painful memories.

Copyright © 1992 by Harcourt Brace Jovanovich, Inc. All rights reserved.

Oh yes it seems to smell awful bad around the front seats we think that's from the gold fish and octopi that we could never find.

Your valued client.

Marshall Meese

Copyright © 1992 by Harcourt Brace Jovanovich, Inc. All rights reserved.

15

Appositives

In sentences you sometimes use a noun whose meaning may not be as clear to your reader as it is to you. For example, suppose that you write:

Estivation is used by some desert animals to survive summer's heat.

If you think that your reader may not know what *estivation* is, you can add a phrase to your sentence to provide more information about estivation.

Estivation, *a slowing down of the body's processes,* is used by some desert animals to survive summer's heat.

This kind of explanatory phrase is called an **appositive** (from the verb *to appose,* meaning "to place things beside each other"). An appositive is a phrase placed beside a noun in order to clarify that noun's meaning. Study the following sentences, in which the appositives have been italicized. Notice that each appositive *immediately follows the noun it describes.*

John Bilson, *the senior senator in Congress,* will be the speaker.
Thursday is named for Thor, *a god of Scandinavian mythology.*

The city of Williamsburg, *the center of Virginia's colonial government*, is now a great tourist attraction.

As you can see, appositives must be set off by commas from the rest of the sentence just as parenthetical expressions are. Appositives are considered *extra* elements in a sentence because they add additional information about a noun that has already been *specifically identified*. For example, in the first sentence above, even without the appositive "the senior senator in Congress," you know which person will be the speaker because he has already been specifically identified as *John Bilson*. In the second sentence, even without the appositive "a god of Scandinavian mythology," the person after whom Thursday is named has already been specifically identified as *Thor*. Similarly, in the third sentence, even without the appositive "a center of Virginia's colonial government," you know that the city which is a great tourist attraction is specifically *Williamsburg*.

Here is the rule for punctuating this kind of explanatory phrase or clause:

If a phrase or clause adds additional information about a noun that has already been specifically identified, that phrase or clause must be completely set off from the rest of the sentence by commas.

In this lesson, you will be dealing with appositives, which are phrases. In Lesson 16, you will be applying the same rule to clauses.

Specifically identified includes mentioning either a person's first or last name, or both, or using words such as "my oldest brother," "my ten o'clock class on Monday," or "my hometown." The nouns in these last three phrases are considered to be *specifically identified* because even though you have not mentioned your brother's name, you can have only one "oldest" brother. Similarly, only one specific town can be your "hometown." In other words, *specifically identified* means limiting the meaning of a general word like *town* to *one particular* town or limiting a general word like *class* to *one particular* class.

Underline the appositives in the following sentences, and then punctuate them. Remember that appositives *follow* the nouns that they describe.

I will leave next Monday the day after my birthday.

English everyone's favorite subject is a required course.

Have you been to our nation's capital Washington, D.C.?

My cousin Pam the only girl in her family wants to coach football.

The plane in the movie was a DC-3 a favorite of many old pilots.

World View a series of tours of ancient civilizations will begin its first tour
in March.

On the other hand, if a phrase is *necessary* to establish the specific identity
of a noun, it is *not* set off by commas. Study the difference between the following pair of sentences.

The novel *Great Expectations* is considered by many critics to be Charles
Dickens' greatest work. (No commas are used to set off *Great Expectations* because the title is necessary to identify which of Dickens' many novels
is considered to be his greatest work.)
Charles Dickens' fourteenth novel, *Great Expectations*, is considered by
many critics to be his greatest work. (Commas are used to set off *Great
Expectations* because Dickens' greatest work has already been specifically
identified as his *fourteenth novel.*)

Most single-word appositives are necessary to establish the specific identity of the nouns they follow and are, therefore, *not* set off by commas.

My sister *Elizabeth* is married to Tim Nolan.
The word *microfiche* means ''a sheet of microfilm.''
Certain tones of the color *red* are known to increase anxiety.

Underline the appositives in the following sentences, and then add commas
wherever they are necessary. Some sentences may not require commas.

Ben Johnson one of the greatest runners in history tarnished his reputation
by using steroids in the 1988 Olympics.

Pitcairn's Island a small dot in the southeastern Pacific Ocean was settled
by a boatload of British mutineers.

My friend Lila has over twenty different books about jewelry.

Kudzu grass a non-native plant in the United States has invaded many areas
of the South and costs millions of dollars to control.

The word *mercurial* comes from the personal traits of the Greek God Mercury.

Pennsylvania is named after William Penn a leader of colonial America.

EXERCISE 15A

Add commas to the following sentences wherever they are necessary. If a sentence needs no additional punctuation, label it *C* for *correct*.

1. My sister a chef at a gourmet restaurant is going to cook my birthday dinner.

2. Cooperstown home of Baseball's Hall of Fame is located in New York State.

3. The word *receive* is one of my spelling demons.

4. My sixth grade teacher Mr. Iglesias changed my life.

5. The class was asked to write a critique of the film *Rain*.

6. Lonnie Ravin my second cousin came to my wedding in shorts and sandals.

7. Don't pick *Rhus radicans* for your bouquet, or you'll be sorry because it's also called by another name poison ivy.

8. The coach bet on his own team The Rochelle Rockets.

9. Your uncle Leon is a big flirt.

10. The number seven will take you to heaven.

11. Deep blue or indigo is her favorite color.

12. She printed the letters *ERA* across the front of her T-shirt.

Copyright © 1992 by Harcourt Brace Jovanovich, Inc. All rights reserved.

13. Thomas A. Edison inventor of the incandescent light conducted thousands of tests before succeeding.

14. Private detectives sometimes called *private eyes* lead very boring lives.

15. She's seen the movie *The Wizard of Oz* thirteen times.

16. They dined on bagels, cream cheese and three pounds of *lox* that is smoked salmon.

Copyright © 1992 by Harcourt Brace Jovanovich, Inc. All rights reserved.

EXERCISE 15B

Add commas and semicolons to the following sentences wherever they are necessary. If a sentence needs no additional punctuation, label it *C* for *correct*. This exercise covers punctuation rules from previous lessons as well as the punctuation of appositives.

1. Computers those remarkable machines are not an unmixed blessing.

2. It is true they have prodigious memories memories much greater than a human's.

3. These prodigious memories however store all those facts about your private life facts you may wish to keep private.

4. These computer memories are not only prodigious they are untiring whatever facts are stored about you will be waiting in those memories when you are old and grey.

5. An enemy of yours could press a button and know all of your secrets your most private of privacies.

6. Computers do sometimes accidentally have accidents and when they do the accidents are lulus far-reaching, devastating accidents.

7. A computer accident can lose all the computer's data forever, can mail out thousands of bad checks to the wrong people, and can even trigger Armageddon a final World War.

Copyright © 1992 by Harcourt Brace Jovanovich, Inc. All rights reserved.

8. Worse than computer accidents are the intentional invasions of computer systems by *hackers* often ruthless and selfish computer freaks.

9. Hackers sneak into the computer networks of public utilities, of our national defense networks, of our private banks.

10. Their power to hurt the rest of us grows from the power of computers themselves.

11. When we can't keep computers out of the hands of knowledgeable hackers we become the victims of our own ingenuity.

12. No machine especially the computer is any more beneficial than the hand that fingers its keys.

Copyright © 1992 by Harcourt Brace Jovanovich, Inc. All rights reserved.

EXERCISE 15C

Part One The sentences below are arranged in pairs. Combine each pair into a third sentence. Use information from the second sentence *to create an appositive in the first sentence*. Decide whether you should set off the appositive with commas. The first pair has been done as an example:

1. a. My brother works for the city.

   b. My brother's name is John.

   c. *My brother John works for the city.*

2. a. My aunt likes pie for dessert.

   b. Her name is Lois.

   c. _____

3. a. John went to mass on Sunday.

   b. Mass is the main service at his church.

   c. _____

4. a. My friend left his job.

   b. He is a staff engineer at Ramco.

   c. _____

5. a. Rita's latest movie is a hit.

   b. The movie is also a critical success.

   c. _____

Copyright © 1992 by Harcourt Brace Jovanovich, Inc. All rights reserved.

6. a. Timmy loves kidney beans.

   b. They are a good source of protein.

   c. _____

7. a. We spent our vacation at Lake Tahoe.

   b. Lake Tahoe is my mom's favorite place.

   c. _____

8. a. The baking soda worked very well.

   b. Baking soda is a product with many uses.

   c. _____

Part Two   Add appositive phrases to the following sentences. If necessary, set off the appositives with commas. The first two sentences have been done as examples.

9. My brother _____ *John* _____ graduated in 1988.

10. Mt. Rushmore, ___ *site of the famous Presidential portraits* ___, in stone is in South Dakota.

11. Among my friends, my friend _____ knows me best.

12. A favorite tourist destination _____ became overcrowded last summer.

13. My birthday month _____ comes at the best time of the year.

14. My uncle _____ gave me his old TV.

15. She likes to visit her hometown _____.

16. The plant _____ causes many allergies.

Copyright © 1992 by Harcourt Brace Jovanovich, Inc. All rights reserved.

16

Restrictive and Nonrestrictive Clauses

In Lesson 15 you learned that if a phrase adds extra information about a noun that has already been specifically identified, that phrase (an **appositive**) must be set off by commas. For example:

Albert Einstein, the great scientist, wrote passionate love letters.

The appositive is set off by commas because the person who wrote passionate love letters has already been specifically identified as Einstein.

On the other hand, if a phrase is *necessary* to establish the specific identity of a noun, the phrase is *not* set off by commas.

The movie *Star Wars* is based on very old legends.

The phrase *Star Wars* is not set off by commas because it is necessary to identify which specific movie is based on very old legends.

The same rule that applies to the punctuation of appositive phrases also applies to the punctuation of *clauses*. Read the following sentences, in which the dependent clauses have been italicized. Can you see why one sentence in each pair has commas while the other does not?

The man *who invented dynamite* established a famous prize for world peace. Alfred Nobel, *who invented dynamite,* established a famous prize for world peace.

A board game *which is based on the private ownership of property* is now very popular in communist China.

The board game of Monopoly, *which is based on the private ownership of property,* is now very popular in communist China.

In the first sentence of each pair, the dependent clause is necessary to establish the specific identity of the noun it follows. This type of clause is called a **restrictive clause** because it *restricts,* or limits, the meaning of the word it describes. For example, in the first sentence if the restrictive clause were removed, the sentence would read:

The man established a famous prize for world peace.

The meaning of this sentence is unclear since there are millions of men in the world, and any one of them might have established a peace prize. But when the clause is added to the sentence, the meaning of the general word *man* is now *restricted,* or limited, to one particular man—*the man who invented dynamite.* Thus, the restrictive clause, "who invented dynamite" establishes the specific identity of the word *man.*

Similarly, in the third sentence above, the clause "which is based on the private ownership of property" identifies *which* game (of all possible games) is now popular in communist China. It restricts the general word *game* to *one particular* game—*the game which is based on the private ownership of property.*

Since restrictive clauses are necessary to establish the specific identity of the nouns they describe, the following punctuation rule applies:

Restrictive clauses are *not* set off by commas.

In contrast, the clauses in the second and fourth sentences are *not* necessary to identify which particular man established a peace prize or which particular game is now popular in communist China. In these sentences, the man has already been specifically identified as *Alfred Nobel,* and the game has already been specifically identified as *Monopoly.* Since these clauses are *not* restrictive clauses, they are called **nonrestrictive clauses**. Nonrestrictive clauses merely add extra information about the nouns they describe. They serve the same function as appositives and are punctuated in the same way.

Nonrestrictive clauses must be completely set off from the rest of the sentence by commas.

This means that if a nonrestrictive clause is at the *end* of a sentence, it will be *preceded* by a comma. If it is in the *middle* of a sentence, it will be *both preceded and followed* by a comma. (Like appositives, nonrestrictive clauses never occur at the beginning of a sentence since they must follow the noun that they describe.)

The restrictive and nonrestrictive clauses that you have been studying are called **adjective clauses** because, like adjectives, these clauses describe nouns. The words that most frequently introduce adjective clauses are:

that
which
who
whom
whose

Like all clauses, adjective clauses must contain both a subject and a verb. But notice that in adjective clauses *the word that introduces the clause may also be the subject of the clause.*

               S   V
George is a man *who works hard.*

Or the clause may contain a separate subject:

                 S   V
The picture *that she drew* showed a child's hand.

Adjective clauses, like adverb clauses (see Lesson 9), are used in **complex sentences.** Although these sentences may not seem to be complex at first glance, if you study the sentences above, you will see that each of them has two subjects and two verbs. Also, if the adjective clause, which is the **dependent clause,** is removed from the sentence, a complete independent clause remains.

                           S   V
INDEPENDENT CLAUSE   George is a man

```
                              S    V
DEPENDENT CLAUSE     who works hard

                              S       V
INDEPENDENT CLAUSE   The picture showed a child's hand

                            S    V
DEPENDENT CLAUSE     that she drew
```

An adjective clause often occurs in the middle of a sentence since it must follow the noun it describes. When an adjective clause is in the middle of a sentence, part of the independent clause precedes it, and the rest of the independent clause follows it. For example:

```
     S         S     V
Switzerland, which trains every single adult male for its army, has avoided
```

war for centuries.

```
     S        S    V       V
The food that she likes most is non-fattening.
```

A sentence may contain more than one adjective clause. Each clause is punctuated separately. In the following sentences, the first adjective clause is *nonrestrictive* (with commas), and the second clause is *restrictive* (no commas).

The banjo, *which was invented by an American,* uses metal strings *that resonate against a drumhead.*
Death Valley, *which is the lowest point in the United States,* has daytime temperatures *that sometimes reach 124 degrees.*

Underline every adjective clause in each of the following sentences, and circle the noun that it describes. Then decide which clauses are restrictive (and do *not* need commas) and which clauses are nonrestrictive (and do need commas). Add the appropriate punctuation.

Note: Although clauses beginning with *who, whom, whose,* or *which* may be either restrictive or nonrestrictive, clauses which begin with *that* are *always* restrictive.

Do you like the present that I gave you?

My father who could repair anything on a car never owned a new car.

She is someone whom Fate has given the looks of a goddess.

The Panama Canal which joins the Atlantic and Pacific Oceans cost the lives of many men.

His uncle Hiram whose wife inherited millions has never done an honest day's work.

Sandra likes men who treat women as equals.

EXERCISE 16A

The essay below includes restrictive and non-restrictive clauses. Add commas and semicolons wherever necessary.

According to an old Chinese legend, a farmer who was called Bobo could do nothing right. Several times, to the amusement of his neighbors, Bobo accidentally burnt down his barn, killing the pig that he prized above all others. One day, after pulling his dead pig from the ashes, Bobo licked his fingers and discovered a surprise, the pig which he had accidentally roasted was delicious. For a while, Bobo burnt down his barn every month because he liked the taste of the roasted pig. One day his wife who was gifted with common sense said to him, ''Bobo, let's leave the barn standing and burn the pig on a smaller fire. It should taste just as good.'' Well, she was right. Today men regard Bobo as history's first cook, but women say it was his wife who deserves that honor.

However it began, cooking food which only humans do is very ancient. As this basic art has developed, two main types have evolved: dry heat cooking and moist heat cooking. The difference between the two processes depends, of course, on the means by

Copyright © 1992 by Harcourt Brace Jovanovich, Inc. All rights reserved.

which heat is transferred to the food that is being cooked. Examples of dry heat processes are broiling, or roasting in a ventilated oven, or on a rotisserie in the air above the fire. Baking is the least "dry" of these methods because the moisture that is released from the food circulates as a warm vapor around the food. Surprisingly, deep-fat frying and sauteeing are dry-heat cooking since the heat is transferred not only through the pan and the fat in the pan but also through the steam that is released from the cooking food.

The principal methods of moist-heat cooking are boiling, pressure cooking, scalding, simmering, poaching, stewing, fricassee, braising, casseroling, cooking in wraps, double boiling and steaming. In all these cases, some liquid which is usually water transfers heat to the food. Of course, some moist-heat recipes, such as some stews, may include a dry-heat stage which usually begins with pan browning of the stew meat.

Many of the methods that cooks have discovered have been happy accidents like Bobo's roast pig. Who cares? Pass me a juicy rib that is covered with lots of sauce. Here's to Bobo and serendipity!

(The information in this discussion comes from the 1975 edition of *The Joy of Cooking*, by Irma S. Rombauer and Marion Rombauer Becker.)

Copyright © 1992 by Harcourt Brace Jovanovich, Inc. All rights reserved.

EXERCISE 16B

To the essay below, add commas and semicolons wherever they are necessary. This exercise covers all lessons we have studied up to now.

Stuttering or technically *dysphemia* is a speech disorder which afflicts many small children. Most children will outgrow the disorder naturally, unfortunately, their anxious parents who are usually embarrassed by their child's faulty speech try to "cure" the stammering. These negative reactions and attempted cures by the parents end up making the disorder even worse and all too often make it permanent.

Stuttering is quite common in two and three year olds the age when children attempt to master speech. For reasons which are not entirely clear, stuttering runs in families and it is more prevalent in boys than in girls.

One pattern that is certain is the relation of stuttering to stress. Stuttering increases with stress in the child's life children often begin to stutter for example when a new baby brother or sister arrives, a time when the stutterer may feel left out or neglected. Some children suddenly start to stutter after the family has moved or after some

Copyright © 1992 by Harcourt Brace Jovanovich, Inc. All rights reserved.

important adult has moved away from the family. Stuttering therefore seems to be an emotional and not a physical disorder.

It is only natural for parents to be concerned about stuttering and to try to cure it however parents who are knowledgeable about stuttering will deal with it indirectly and not by directly saying to the child words like "Stop, and speak correctly!" They will ignore the times when the child stutters and instead will try to identify and alleviate whatever emotional conditions are causing the child to be so tense, for instance if someone that the stuttering child loves has suddenly moved away a special effort will be made to spend extra time with the child.

Soon the child will resume speaking smoothly and clearly the parents who suffer with their child will have saved the child from the anguish of the chronic stutterer.

(The information in this discussion comes from the current edition of *Doctor Spock's Baby and Child Care* by Benjamin Spock, M.D. and Michael Rothenberg, M.D. and from the 1975 edition of *The New Columbia Encyclopedia*.)

Copyright © 1992 by Harcourt Brace Jovanovich, Inc. All rights reserved.

EXERCISE 16C

Part One   Construct complex sentences of your own using the words listed below to form *restrictive* clauses. Underline the adjective clause in each of your sentences, and circle the noun it describes.

1. that: _____

_____

2. who: _____

_____

3. which: _____

_____

4. whose: _____

_____

Part Two   Construct complex sentences of your own using the words listed below to form *nonrestrictive* clauses. Underline the adjective clause in each of your sentences, and circle the noun it describes. Use appropriate punctuation.

5. which: _____

_____

6. who: _____

_____

7. whose: _____

_____

Copyright © 1992 by Harcourt Brace Jovanovich, Inc. All rights reserved.

8. whom: _____

_____

Part Three Underline the adjective clauses in the following sentences, and circle the word which each clause describes. If the clause is nonrestrictive, add the necessary punctuation. If the clause is restrictive, the sentence needs no additional punctuation, so label it *C* for *correct*.

9. A person who knows how to boil water isn't necessarily a good maker of coffee.

10. In fact, coffee which has been boiled tends to be bitter and cloudy because boiling brings out tannic acid from the bean.

11. Good coffee begins with good coffee beans.

12. Beans that are ground at home should be ground fresh each time in a clean grinder.

13. South American beans which probably come from Brazil or Colombia have much more caffeine than those grown in Puerto Rico.

14. Beans ought to be stored air tight in the refrigerator.

15. Today's shoppers will find in their markets excellent ground coffee that has been vacuum packed or freeze dried.

16. Study the manufacturer's directions which should be followed carefully; any of these methods—drip, percolated, or steeped—will result in a cup of coffee that will please any palate.

17. With any method that you use, always start with a scrupulously clean coffee maker that has been rinsed in a solution of baking soda water and scalded just before use.

Copyright © 1992 by Harcourt Brace Jovanovich, Inc. All rights reserved.

17

Items in a Series and Dates and Addresses

A **series** consists of *three or more* related items. Commas are placed between each item in a series in order to separate the items from each other. The final comma before the conjunction is optional.

Jogging, dancing, and singing are three activities she loves.

or

Jogging, dancing and singing are three activities she loves.

If *every* item in a series is joined by a conjunction (*and, or,* or *nor*), no commas are needed since the conjunctions keep the individual items separated. This type of construction is used only when the writer wishes to place particular emphasis on the number of items in the series.

The cost of college may include tuition and books and transportation.

If a date or an address consists of more than one item, a comma is used after each part of the date or the address, *including a comma after the last item.* (If the last item in the series is also the last word in the sentence, only a period follows it.) Notice that this punctuation rule differs from the rule used for punctuating an ordinary series.

February 12, 1809, was the birthday of Abraham Lincoln.

The name of a month and the number of the day (February 12) are considered a single item and are separated from the year by a comma. However, notice that a comma also *follows* 1809, which is the last item in the date.

The old Chisholm Trail from San Antonio, Texas, to Abilene, Kansas, was used to move cattle from the range to railroad depots.

Notice the commas after "Texas" and "Kansas." These commas are used in addition to the commas that separate the names of the cities from the names of the states.

If a date or an address consists of only a single item, no comma is necessary.

February 14 is Valentine's Day.
I have lived in both Michigan and California.

A comma is not used before a Zip Code number.

The mailing address for Hollywood is Los Angeles, California 90028.

Punctuate the following sentences:

Every mini-mall in the neighborhood has a frozen yogurt shop a Chinese restaurant and a VCR store.

His professor lectured answered questions and gave the test.

If you drive fifty-five miles per hour, you can go from Long Island New York to Los Angeles California in six or seven days.

Louella wants ham with gravy and coffee with cream.

Jackie resides at 904 Adams Street Mercer Idaho 70413.

EXERCISE 17A

Add commas to the following sentences wherever they are needed. If a sentence needs no additional punctuation, label it *C* for *correct*. This exercise covers only the punctuation of items in a series and dates and addresses.

1. I always send my mother a card on the sixth of April.

2. Our train will leave from San Diego California and two days later deposit us in Topeka Kansas.

3. Francine is quite tall quite blonde and quite dangerous. (Notice that adjective and adverbs, like nouns, may be in a series.)

4. I capped off the banquet by consuming three crepes suzette with brandy sauce and a cup of tea with lemon.

5. I would rather visit Miami Beach in Florida than go to Philadelphia Pennsylvania.

6. Madonna stretched toward the ceiling arched right and left and bowed to her audience.

7. Electra received a dozen brownies on Valentine's Day.

8. Kenny was accompanied by his sister and brother and by Lester and Myra Hall.

9. Don't forget July 4 1776 or December 7 1941.

10. The package from London England should arrive after the fifteenth of June.

Copyright © 1992 by Harcourt Brace Jovanovich, Inc. All rights reserved.

11. She had worked for a lawyer for a dentist and for a women's clothing store.

12. The letters *E R* and *A* stand for *Equal* and **Rights** and *Amendment.*

13. Get in touch with her at Suite 904 Tower Building 303 Adams Street Lindenville Ohio 86929.

14. Gary or Frank or Ed or Benjamin will be best man.

15. Go on July Fourth to Sylvan Park on Sylvan Boulevard.

Copyright © 1992 by Harcourt Brace Jovanovich, Inc. All rights reserved.

EXERCISE 17B

Add semicolons and commas wherever they are necessary in the following letter. This exercise covers all of the lessons on punctuation that we have studied.

January 3, 1991

Mr. Dale Bryant
Liqui-Pro Corporation
Beesville, Kentucky

Dear Mr. Bryant:

You have asked me to detail the reasons that I think would make me a good sales manager for your firm. Let me describe my selling experience to you.

On my seventeenth birthday May 19 1988 I began work as a salesman with Joyner Motors in Teeson Alabama. Within six months I was their top salesperson, sometimes selling as many as six units per week. Nellie Jones my sales manager's secretary used to tell me over lunch that she'd never seen ''a salesman who could touch you Slick!'' But without any warning and with no letter of recommendation, her boss fired me on April 3 of 1989.

I moved to Alston Georgia the next week and began selling for the Lee Waterbed Company. Although I soon became their best

Copyright © 1992 by Harcourt Brace Jovanovich, Inc. All rights reserved.

salesman I was suddenly fired on November 10 1989. When I went to pick up my VCR from Jenny Lee who was the boss' daughter she told me, "Earl my daddy thinks you are a great salesman but he doesn't like your style."

I moved that week here to Barter Kentucky where I sell women's lingerie. I am doing very well here as top salesman but Jill Jepson whose husband owns Dain-Tee Duds has mentioned to me that her husband thinks, "That super-salesman (that's me) has outlived his usefulness!"

As you can see Mr. Bryant I can sell anything however I can't seem to get along with my superiors. That's why I thought if I started *at the top* as your sales manager I could make you lots of money and have a long productive career with your firm.

Sincerely

Earl "Slick" Pearson

Copyright © 1992 by Harcourt Brace Jovanovich, Inc. All rights reserved.

EXERCISE 17C

Add semicolons and commas wherever they are necessary in the following letter. This exercise covers all of the lessons on punctuation that we have studied.

In elementary school I was a skinny girl who always received valentines on Valentine's Day. When I was in sixth grade my mother and I moved from California to Liston Iowa a small town where my mother had grown up. My father stayed in California I missed his voice which I remembered so clearly saying, "Time for pancakes, Barbie darling."

After I entered Liston Junior High in the seventh grade I grew to be 5'7''. After that I continued to grow outward. I sat around reading watching TV and eating. Fritos and pizza which were my specialty wouldn't last a day in our house. I was soon quite overweight and was teased at school. Though I had bright green eyes, nice hair, and knew I was a decent person I had no social life whatsoever. My few friends were other unpopular students and needless to say no boy ever looked twice at me because I was not foxy. Of course most other students were not either.

Copyright © 1992 by Harcourt Brace Jovanovich, Inc. All rights reserved.

For years my mother nagged me every time I stuffed myself then a counselor convinced mother to enroll me in a free summer program that was sponsored by the Public Health Department for overweight people. I returned to school in September of this year many pounds lighter. My mother and I spent a week buying clothes for me to wear my senior year.

Although my specialist had prepared me that first week of school was a shock. I was still somewhat heavy but evidently I was now more attractive to men however I had no practice in coping with all the men who began to talk to me. I became worried some at first about this problem but I kept up my confidence and stayed determined.

In our Public Health Department program we had many overweight women come to speak to us. They were successful women good mothers and working women and fine people. Some owned businesses and moved freely in the business world, they reinforced my self-esteem and taught our class many techniques for coping. Here at school I have already reached out to two girls who had questions about my weight loss I told them about my experience in the free program and gave them the phone number. It changed my life. I'm still "recovering" but I'm in charge.

Copyright © 1992 by Harcourt Brace Jovanovich, Inc. All rights reserved.

Review of Punctuation that
"Sets Off" or Separates

Add commas and semicolons (no periods) to the following sentences wherever they are necessary.

This story was told in the Middle Ages a cold and violent time.

Three men were gambling and drinking late one night in a small town. They noticed a stranger at the tavern who seemed to be wealthy. The three men were friendly to the stranger and bought him drinks but when they all left the tavern together the three men stabbed the stranger, took his money and left him dead.

One of the murderers the oldest said, "Let's go out of town to the spring where we can build a fire and sit down to divide our money all these gold and silver coins."

So they went to the spring and built a fire. Then one of them the youngest murderer said, "While you two count our money, I'll go back and get more to drink a nice cask of ale."

He got up and walked away while the other two spread out the coins which glistened gold and silver in the firelight. "You know," said the oldest murderer, "I have never liked that young fellow. I hope he falls and cracks his skull."

Copyright © 1992 by Harcourt Brace Jovanovich, Inc. All rights reserved.

"Well friend we could crack it for him when he gets back," said the other.

"Yes of course then the money that he would get will come to the two who deserve it most you and me."

Meanwhile the youngest had bought a cask of ale and started back. As he walked along he thought to himself, "Why should those two cutthroats get any gold and silver? It was *my* idea to kill that stranger." So he got some poison that he had been saving for rats and put it in the cask of ale to kill his two companions.

What more is there to say? When the youngest returned to the fire, the oldest struck him with a rock while the other cut his throat with the same bloody knife that had earlier killed the stranger. After the youngest murderer lay dead upon the ground, the other two sat down to re-divide the gold and silver. First however they celebrated with a drink from the cask of ale which the youngest had carried back to them.

"Money is the root of all evil."

So ends the story which Geoffrey Chaucer told many centuries ago in *The Canterbury Tales*.

Copyright © 1992 by Harcourt Brace Jovanovich, Inc. All rights reserved.

PRONOUN USAGE

18

Subject, Object, and Possessive Pronouns

Pronouns are words that are used to refer to persons, places, things, and ideas without repeating their names. In other words, pronouns are used in place of nouns. For example, rather than saying "Mark bought a new pen only yesterday, but Mark has already lost the pen," you can say, "Mark bought a new pen only yesterday, but *he* has already lost *it*." In this sentence, the pronoun *he* replaces *Mark,* and the pronoun *it* replaces *pen.* The noun that the pronoun replaces is called the **antecedent** (Latin for "to go before") of the pronoun.

There are several different kinds of pronouns, but in this lesson you will be studying only **subject pronouns, object pronouns,** and **possessive pronouns.**

Singular Pronouns	*Subject*	*Object*	*Possessive*
	I	me	my, mine
	you	you	your, yours
	he	him	his
	she	her	her, hers
	it	it	its

Plural Pronouns	*Subject*	*Object*	*Possessive*
	we	us	our, ours
	you	you	your, yours
	they	them	their, theirs

As their name suggests, **subject pronouns** are used as the *subject* of a sentence or a clause. For example:

She is a vice-president at General Dynamics.
They live in the apartment upstairs.

In *formal* speech and writing, subject pronouns are also used after forms of the verb *be,* as in:

That is *he* at the door.
It is *I.*
If I were *she,* I'd take the job.

In formal speech and writing, subject pronouns are used after forms of the verb *be* because they refer to the *same* thing or person as the subject.

That = *he* at the door.
It = *I.*
If I = *she,* I'd take the job.

However, in *informal* speech, many people would use object pronouns in the sentences below.

That is (or *That's*) *him* at the door.
It is (or *It's*) *me.*
If I were *her,* I'd take the job.

Whether you choose to say "it is I" or "it is me" depends upon the circumstances. If you are taking an English test or writing a formal essay, using subject pronouns after forms of *be* is appropriate and expected. But if you are speaking casually with a friend, "it is I" may sound artificial, and the informal "it is me" might be more suitable.

In this unit, you will be studying both grammar and usage. Try to keep clear in your mind those situations in which you have a choice between formal and informal constructions (usage) and those situations in which only one pronoun form is correct at all times (grammar).

"It is *she*" versus "It is *her*" = usage.
"Al and *I* are here" versus "Al and *me* are here" = grammar.

Object pronouns are used as objects of prepositions, as direct objects, and as indirect objects.

You will remember that the noun or pronoun in a prepositional phrase is called the **object of the preposition.** That is why an object pronoun replaces the noun. For example:

The report was sent to *Marie.*
The report was sent to *her.*
The cheerleader yelled at the *fans.*
The cheerleader yelled at *them.*

Object pronouns are also used as direct objects. A **direct object** is the word that *receives* the action of the verb and, with very few exceptions, follows the verb, often as the next word.

The teacher tested the *students.*
   (subject)   (direct object)

The teacher tested *them.*

She liked *Frank* immediately.
(subject)   (direct object)

She liked *him* immediately.

Another way in which object pronouns are used is as indirect objects. An **indirect object** is the person or thing *to whom* or *for whom* something is done.

They awarded the *winner* a prize.
(subject)   (indirect   (direct
             object)   object)

They awarded *her* a prize.

The previous sentence is another way of saying, "They awarded a prize *to her*."

Lonnie bought his *sister* a new album.
(subject)   (indirect   (direct
                          object)   object)

Lonnie bought *her* a new album.

The previous sentence is another way of saying, "Lonnie bought a new album *for her*."

Possessive pronouns are used to show ownership.

The tiger licked *its* paw.
The men shaved *their* beards after the contest.

Very few people make pronoun errors when there is only one subject or one object in a sentence. For example, no native speaker of English would say, "Me am here" instead of "I am here." However, people often do make mistakes when two subjects or two objects are paired up in a sentence. For example, which of the following two sentences is grammatically correct?

Mrs. Jones invited my husband and *me* to her party.
Mrs. Jones invited my husband and *I* to her party.

To determine the correct pronoun in this kind of "double" construction, split the sentence in two like this:

1. Mrs. Jones invited my husband to her party.
2. Mrs. Jones invited (me, I) to her party.

As you can tell after you have split the sentence in two, it would be incorrect to say "Mrs. Jones invited *I* to her party." The correct pronoun is *me,* which is the direct object of the verb *invited.* Therefore, the whole sentence should read:

Mrs. Jones invited my husband and *me* to her party.

Which of the following two sentences is correct?

Janet mailed Lorne and *I* the package.
Janet mailed Lorne and *me* the package.

Again, split the sentences in two.

1. Janet mailed Lorne the package.
2. Janet mailed (I, me) the package.

Now, which pronoun is correct?

Another very common pronoun error is using subject pronouns instead of object pronouns after prepositions. The object of a preposition must be an *object* pronoun. Which of the following two sentences is correct?

The teacher returned the test to Ken and *I.*
The teacher returned the test to Ken and *me.*

If you split the sentence in two, you have:

1. The teacher returned the test to Ken.
2. The teacher returned the test to (I, me).

The correct pronoun is *me,* which is the object of the preposition *to.* Therefore, the correct sentence is:

The teacher returned the test to Ken and *me.*

It is extremely important that you do not decide which pronoun to use simply on the basis of what ''sounds better'' *unless you split the sentence in two first.* To many people, ''Mrs. Jones invited my husband and *I* to her party'' sounds more ''correct'' than ''Mrs. Jones invited my husband and *me* to her party''; yet, as you have seen, *me* is actually the correct pronoun.

Another example of choosing an incorrect pronoun because it ''sounds better'' is the frequent misuse of the subject pronoun *I* after the preposition *between.* As you already know, the object of a preposition must be an *object* pronoun. Therefore, it is always incorrect to say 'between you and *I.*'' The *correct* construction is ''between you and *me.*''

Circle the pronoun that correctly completes each of the following sentences.

It should be divided between you and (I, me).

They warned our friends and (we, us) about prowlers.

My uncle and (he, him) ride the same bus.

The coach gave the team and (I, me) another chance.

The award is for you and (she, her).

Occasionally you may use constructions like the following:

Does the new law concern *us women?*
We voters must elect good leaders.

To determine whether the sentence requires a subject or an object pronoun, see which pronoun would be correct if the pronoun appeared in the sentence by itself rather than being followed by a noun.

Does the new law concern (us, we) women? =
Does the new law concern (we, us)?
(We, us) voters must elect responsible candidates. =
(We, us) must elect responsible candidates.
The correct pronouns are *us* women and *we* voters.

Circle the pronoun that correctly completes each of the following sentences.

It is not for (we, us) relatives to settle the argument.

(We, us) club members should publish a newsletter.

EXERCISE 18A

The first part of this exercise is intended for a quick review of subject and object pronouns. Reverse each sentence so that the subject pronoun becomes the object and the object pronoun becomes the subject.

Example: *I* waited for *them.*
Answer: *They* waited for *me.*

   1. *We* wrote *them* last month.

   2. *You* gave *her* too much money.

   3. *She* sent the picture to *them.*

   4. *They* relied on *us* for help.

   5. *He* liked *you* so much.

   6. *He* baked *her* a valentine.

   7. *She* sent one card to *her* each Monday.

   8. *It* sought *them* in the underbrush.

Circle the pronoun that correctly completes each sentence. Remember to split the sentence if it contains a "double" construction. Apply the rules of formal English usage.

   9. Jack and (him, he) are old friends.

  10. It is (she, her) who should be grateful.

  11. Amanda and (him, he) like the same music.

Copyright © 1992 by Harcourt Brace Jovanovich, Inc. All rights reserved.

12. Will it be (them, they) at the airport?

13. Larry and (she, her) are back together.

14. The choice was vetoed by (we, us) members.

15. The gang were shocked by (him, he) and his actions.

16. Do you know who made this for Sara and (him, he)?

17. The loss of (we, us) veterans hurt the team.

18. Those principles were advocated by (them, they) and us.

19. The former treasurer and (she, her) were tied in the election.

20. Give a second chance to (us, we) late bloomers.

Copyright © 1992 by Harcourt Brace Jovanovich, Inc. All rights reserved.

EXERCISE 18B

Some of the following sentences contain pronoun errors. Cross out the incorrect pronouns, and write in the correct forms. If a sentence contains no pronoun errors, label it *C* for *correct*. Apply the rules of formal English usage.

1. John will appoint four of we former members to the committee.

2. They observed Jackson and he at the raid.

3. After us reporters took our pictures, the bridge collapsed.

4. Neither Gracie nor him will give in.

5. The first to finish were Neeley and her.

6. He will come to George and him for help.

7. Us users of the gym were asked to bring our own towels.

8. Next year their team and we will party after the game.

9. Mike and she will enjoy the movie.

10. Just between you and I, the boss is a nerd.

11. The answer surprised Thomas and her.

12. The reunion attracted most of us ex-jocks.

13. You surprised Phoebe and we with your present.

14. The cooperation between Marcie and them was heartening.

15. Will you review the test for Jerry and I?

Copyright © 1992 by Harcourt Brace Jovanovich, Inc. All rights reserved.

16. The plan succeeded because of Harry and them.

17. We left Annie with Bruce and he after lunch.

18. The tent was located between the old couple in the Ford and we Wilsons in our Chevy pickup.

19. He needed Frank and I to help him.

20. Fortunately, between you, with your concern, and he, with his feeling of friendship, this disagreement can be settled.

Copyright © 1992 by Harcourt Brace Jovanovich, Inc. All rights reserved.

EXERCISE 18C

Part One   Give the following sentences two subjects by adding a subject pronoun to each sentence. *Use a different pronoun for each sentence.* Apply the rules of formal English usage. The first sentence has been done as an example.

           and she
1. Those people upstairs ∧ are neighbors.

2. The leader left early.

3. My dog ran after Grandma's car.

4. Her canaries almost froze.

5. Her Aunt Kathy knew the answer.

6. The actor's nose were blurred in the photograph.

7. Jonathan knows better.

Part Two   Give the following sentences two objects by adding an object pronoun to each sentence. *Use a different object pronoun for each sentence.* Apply the rules of formal English usage. The first sentence has been done as an example.

          and him
8. She wrote Terri ∧ last week.

9. She left with Tony for work.

10. The oldest player outscored Nellie.

11. Harriet wrote to the Lorco Corporation.

12. Her house was decorated by Charley.

Copyright © 1992 by Harcourt Brace Jovanovich, Inc. All rights reserved.

13. The out-of-control truck threatened the little boy.

14. The cake for Paul soon disappeared.

15. She arrived with Isaac at the last minute.

Copyright © 1992 by Harcourt Brace Jovanovich, Inc. All rights reserved.

19

Pronouns in Comparisons and Pronouns with -self, -selves

Using Pronouns in Comparisons

In speech and in writing, we often compare two people or two things with each other. For example:

Marcia is wiser than *I* am.
The mechanic charged *Ike* more than he charged *me*.

In the sentences above, it is easy to tell whether a subject pronoun or an object pronoun should be used in each comparison. In the first sentence, the subject pronoun *I* is correct because it would be clearly ungrammatical to say that "Marcia is wiser than *me* am." In the second sentence, the object pronoun *me* is correct because you would not say that "The mechanic charged Ike more than he charged *I*."

However, people usually do not write out their comparisons completely. They use a shortened form instead. For example:

Tammy cooks better than *I.*
The film impressed *Don* more than *me.*

In these cases, it is possible to determine which pronoun is correct by mentally filling in the words that have been left out of the comparison.

Tammy cooks better than I (do).
The film impressed Don more than (it impressed) me.

Fill in the missing words to determine which pronouns are correct in the following sentences.

My co-worker deserves more praise than (I, me).

Making good grades is harder for Ed than (I, me).

His family reads less than (we, us).

The news shocked you more than (he, him).

When you fill in the missing words, the correct comparisons are:

My co-worker deserves more praise than *I* (do).
Making good grades is harder for Ed than (it is for) *me.*
His family reads less than *we* (do).
The news shocked you more than (it shocked) *him.*

In *informal* usage, you often hear people use object pronouns instead of subject pronouns in comparisons. (For example, "He's taller than me" instead of "He's taller than I.") However, these forms are generally considered inappropriate in writing and formal speech. You should be especially careful in situations where the wrong pronoun can change the meaning of the entire sentence. For example, "Mary danced with George more than *I* (danced with him)" does not mean the same thing as "Mary danced with George more than (she danced with) *me.*" In addition, using the wrong pronoun can sometimes lead to unintentionally ridiculous sentences, such as:

My husband likes cake more than me.

Unless the husband happens to like food more than he likes his wife, the correct pronoun would be:

My husband likes cake more than *I* (do).

(Note: The conjunction *than,* which is used in comparisons, should not be confused with the adverb *then.*)

Avoiding Doubled Subjects

Do not "double," or repeat, the subject of a sentence by repeating the noun in its pronoun form.

INCORRECT	My friend, she never pays attention.
CORRECT	My friend never pays attention.
INCORRECT	Those new models, they break down easily.
CORRECT	Those new models break down easily.

Pronouns with -self, -selves

Some pronouns end in *-self* or *-selves:*

Singular	*Plural*
myself	ourselves
yourself	yourselves
himself	themselves
herself	
itself	

These pronouns can be used in two ways. They can be reflexive pronouns. **Reflexive pronouns** are used when the object of the verb or the object of the preposition is the same person or thing as the subject. For example:

I touched *myself.* (myself = I)
Greg teaches *himself.* (himself = Greg)
Helen could look at *herself.* (herself = Helen)

Or they may be used for *emphasis.*

The judge *herself* said they were innocent.

Did you build the whole house *yourself*?

We *ourselves* were responsible for the crash.

Notice that the singular forms of reflexive pronouns end in *self*, and the plural forms end in *selves*. In standard English, there are no such forms as *hisself*, *ourselfs*, *theirselfs*, or *themselfs*. These forms are considered nonstandard in both speech and writing and should be avoided unless you are using a dialect, such as you might do in writing a story.

In formal English, the reflexive pronoun *myself* is not used in place of a subject or an object pronoun.

INCORRECT	Jack and *myself* will meet you at 8:00.
CORRECT	Jack and *I* will meet you at 8:00.
INCORRECT	This present is for Alice and *myself*.
CORRECT	This present is for Alice and *me*.

Myself is sometimes used as a subject or an object pronoun in informal usage, but even in these cases the use of the correct subject or object pronoun is preferred. Referring to yourself as *myself* rather than as *I* or *me* does *not* make you sound more polite or more modest.

EXERCISE 19A

Circle the pronoun that most logically and correctly completes each sentence. Apply the rules of formal English usage.

1. Her boyfriend is a better cook than (her, she).

2. The report was about Duane and (myself, me).

3. Gary and (him, he) are old friends.

4. Since both of them played exceptionally well, the MVP went to (her, she) and him.

5. Rachel or (myself, I) will be maid of honor.

6. Meeting the standards is easier for Luella than (I, me).

7. Have the coach and (they, them) agreed on strategy?

8. Harry has been paying a lower rent than (her, she).

9. It was Tony (hisself, himself) who ordered the pizza.

10. The cheesecake is for Alex and (myself, me).

11. Tanya is not any prettier than (I, me).

12. The coach is more biased against Roger than (me, I).

13. My wife likes Thai food more than (him, he).

14. Vivien always eats more hot fudge sundaes than (we, us).

Copyright © 1992 by Harcourt Brace Jovanovich, Inc. All rights reserved.

15. They wrapped the presents for their grandfather (thyselfs, themselves).

16. Rafael tangoed with Alicia, his sister, more often than (me, I), his wife.

17. Iris (she, herself) doesn't like her own cooking.

18. The owner of the car and (I, myself) will meet you at noon.

19. We got good news from them about (ourselves, us).

20. The council elected the candidate who had better qualifications than (I, me).

Copyright © 1992 by Harcourt Brace Jovanovich, Inc. All rights reserved.

EXERCISE 19B

In the essay below cross out the pronoun errors and replace them with the correct forms. This exercise covers this lesson and the previous lesson.

People say the Japanese make better cars and better everything else than us. I myself don't agree with that idea.

If you want to talk about cars, how come the Japanese don't make any cars as large as a Cadillac or a Lincoln? I believe if I were making only mid-size or small compact cars, I could build in as much quality as the Japanese theirselfs do. After all, in a smaller car you spend less on materials, so you could spend more on careful workmanship. We Americans seem to do the opposite.

My dad says, ''The Japanese, they don't need big cars like ourselves, so they build them smaller.'' Well, I understand that. However, I don't see why big Japanese companies, they couldn't go to a little extra trouble and make a car big enough for a tall guy like myself.

There's another thing. I've never been to Japan, but I have friends here in the U.S. who have relatives in Japan. They tell me that the

Copyright © 1992 by Harcourt Brace Jovanovich, Inc. All rights reserved.

whole Japanese culture is much more quality-conscious than us Americans. They have told me horror stories about cousins who committed suicide from not passing a school exam or about mid-level executives killing theirselves because you failed a quota. These stories sound exaggerated, but if its true, that's a high price to pay for quality.

Also I hear that American unions don't like everything about the Japanese style of management-labor relations. I say if they can have people in a company get along better than us, let's try it. There is a lot more to this question of quality than leather seats in a car.

Copyright © 1992 by Harcourt Brace Jovanovich, Inc. All rights reserved.

20

Agreement of Pronouns with Their Antecedents

Agreement in Number

Like nouns, pronouns may be either singular or plural, depending upon whether they refer to one or to more than one person or thing. Following are the subject, object, and possessive pronouns you have learned, divided into singular and plural categories.

Singular Pronouns	*Subject*	*Object*	*Possessive*
	I	me	my, mine
	you	you	your, yours
	he	him	his
	she	her	her, hers
	it	it	its

Plural Pronouns	*Subject*	*Object*	*Possessive*
	we	us	our, ours
	you	you	your, yours
	they	them	their, theirs

Just as a subject must agree in number with its verb, a pronoun must agree in number with its **antecedent.** (The antecedent, you will remember, is the noun to which the pronoun refers.) In other words, if the antecedent is *singular,* the pronoun must be *singular.* If the antecedent is *plural,* the pronoun must be *plural.*

Study the following sentences, in which both the pronouns and their antecedents have been italicized.

> After the *man* wrote the letter, *he* mailed it.
> After the *men* wrote the letter, *they* mailed it.

Obviously, few people would make pronoun agreement errors in the above sentences since *man* is clearly singular, and *men* is clearly plural. However, people often make pronoun agreement errors in cases like the following:

> INCORRECT   A *driver* should reduce *their* speed in bad weather.
> CORRECT   A *driver* should reduce *his* speed in bad weather.

Since drivers include females as well as males, it would be equally correct to say:

> A driver should reduce *her* speed in bad weather.
> A driver should reduce *his* or *her* speed in bad weather.

For a more detailed discussion of the *his or her* construction, see the section on "Avoiding Sexist Language" on page 212.

Notice the differences in these sentences.

> INCORRECT   Each *person* is entitled to *their* own locker.
> CORRECT   Each *person* is entitled to *his* own locker.

What causes people to make mistakes like these? The mistakes may occur because when a writer describes a *driver*, he or she is thinking of drivers (plural) in general. Similarly, a writer may think of a *person* as people in general. Nevertheless, since *driver* and *person* are singular nouns, they must be used with singular pronouns.

Notice that if several pronouns refer to the same antecedent, *all* of the pronouns must agree in number with that antecedent.

If *Nancy* expects higher grades, *she* should do all *her* work.
When the *tourists* leave, *they* take *their* memories with *them.*

Another common pronoun agreement error involves **indefinite pronouns.**
As you learned in Lesson 7 on subject—verb agreement (p. 71), indefinite pronouns are *singular* and require *singular* verbs. (For example, "Everyone *is*
here," *not* "Everyone *are* here.") Similarly, when indefinite pronouns are used
as antecedents, they require *singular* subject, object, and possessive pronouns.

The following words are singular indefinite pronouns.

anybody, anyone, anything
each, each one
either, neither
everybody, everyone, everything
nobody, no one, nothing
somebody, someone, something

Notice the use of singular pronouns with these words.

Everyone did as he pleased.
Somebody has forgotten *her* shawl.
Either of the choices has *its* disadvantages.

In informal spoken English, plural pronouns are often used with indefinite
pronoun antecedents. However, this construction is generally not considered
appropriate in formal speech or writing.

INFORMAL   *Somebody* wants *their* lawyer to phone *them.*
FORMAL   *Somebody* wants *his* lawyer to phone *him.*

In some sentences, an indefinite pronoun is so clearly plural in meaning
that a singular pronoun sounds awkward with it. For example:

Everyone on this block must be wealthy because he drives a Cadillac or
a Mercedes.

A better wording for this sentence would be:

All the people on this block must be wealthy because they all drive a Cadillac or a Mercedes.

Avoiding Sexist Language

Although the matching of singular pronouns with singular antecedents is a grammatical problem, a usage problem may occur if the antecedent of a singular pronoun refers to both sexes. In the past, singular masculine pronouns were used to refer to antecedents such as *person* or *driver* even if these antecedents included women as well as men. Now, many writers prefer to use forms that include both sexes, such as *he or she* or *his or her* in order to avoid excluding females.

Every student should turn his or her papers in on time.
If anyone has seen the missing child, he or she should call the police immediately.

A simpler way is to make both the pronoun and its antecedent plural.

All *students* should turn in *their* papers on time.

Avoiding sexist language is a problem of usage, not of grammar. In order to simplify the rules for you while you are still studying grammar, most of the exercises in this unit will offer you the choice between one singular pronoun (either masculine or feminine) and one plural pronoun. For example:

Everyone should do (her, their) best on the job.
Each parent is responsible for (his, their) own children.

Which pronouns would be correct in the following sentences according to the rules of formal English usage?

If a person wants to lose weight, (he, they) should eat less and exercise more.
A surgeon may spend seven or eight hours on (her, their) feet during a complex operation.
Anyone who knows the answer should raise (their, his) hand.
A good pilot knows (their, her) airplane.
Each of the groups has (its, their) instructions.

Agreement in Person

In grammar, pronouns are classified into groups called **persons. First person** refers to the person who is speaking. **Second person** is the person being spoken to. **Third person** is the person or thing being spoken about. Below is a chart of subject pronouns grouped according to person.

	Singular	*Plural*
first person	I	we
second person	you	you
third person	he, she, it	they

All nouns are considered third person (either singular or plural) because nouns can be replaced by third-person pronouns (for example, *Bob = he; a book = it; apples = they*).

Just as a pronoun and its antecedent must agree in number, they must also agree in person. Agreement in person becomes a problem only when the second-person pronoun *you* is incorrectly used with a third-person antecedent. Study the following examples.

INCORRECT   If *anyone* is allergic to pollen, *you* should avoid the source.
CORRECT   If *anyone* is allergic to pollen, *he* should avoid the source.
INCORRECT   When *voters* go to the polls, *you* should receive your ballot stub.
CORRECT   When *voters* go to the polls, *they* should receive their ballot stubs.

This type of mistake is called a **shift in person** and is considered a serious grammatical error.

In addition to avoiding shifts in person within individual sentences, you should try to be consistent in your use of person when you are writing essays. In general, an entire essay is written in the same person. If, for example, you are writing an essay about the special problems faced by students who work full-time, you will probably use either the first or the third person. You should avoid shifts into the second person (*you*) since *you* refers to the reader of your paper and not to the students you are writing about.

INCORRECT   *Students* who take too many units must often drop classes later in the semester. When *you* register, *you* should plan realistically for the amount of time *you* can allocate to *your* classes and homework.

CORRECT   *Students* who take too many units must often drop classes during the semester. When *they* register, *they* should plan realistically for the amount of time *they* can allocate to *their* classes and homework.

Circle the pronoun that correctly completes each sentence.

Please listen carefully; (your, his, their) full attention is required.

Many states now have no-fault auto insurance for all drivers so that (you, he, they) do not need to go to court to settle (your, his, their) accident claims.

If a person wants to run for office, (they, you, she) must be known to the voters.

EXERCISE 20A

Circle the pronouns that correctly complete each sentence. Apply the rules of formal English usage.

1. (He, Him) and she are best friends.

2. Everyone who heard about the new tax was as angry as (me, I).

3. Someone on the tour lost (their, her) car keys.

4. After I worked harder than (she, her), they gave the job to Geri.

5. When the patients see (their, your) X-rays, they understand the diagnosis.

6. Her prize was announced much sooner than (his, he).

7. The new rules were approved quickly by the renters (themselves, theirselves).

8. Since Hal and (her, she) have lived together, they have never fought.

9. Either the boss or the foreman will give you a lift in (their, his) car.

10. When a tenant is unhappy, (he, you) should go to the manager.

11. Split the check between John and (I, me).

12. If someone needs help, (she, you, they) can call this number.

13. No one should expect (their, her) efforts to go unrewarded.

Copyright © 1992 by Harcourt Brace Jovanovich, Inc. All rights reserved.

14. Anyone who pays his income tax late should file a "Request for Late Filing" form including a check for (their, his, your) tax owed; (they, you, she, he) must be sure to date the form correctly.

15. Were the Andersons and (they, them) good friends?

Copyright © 1992 by Harcourt Brace Jovanovich, Inc. All rights reserved.

EXERCISE 20B

If a sentence contains an error in pronoun usage, cross out the incorrect pronoun, and write in the correct form. Some sentences contain more than one error. If a sentence contains no pronoun errors, label it *C* for *correct*. Apply the rules of formal English usage.

1. Mary's strength is her confidence in herself.

2. The obstacle was more difficult for the quarterback than her.

3. If Ronald keeps his cool, the authorities won't condemn his property.

4. Someone in the room is about to be scared out of your socks.

5. Our class' teacher was wiser than him.

6. If a customer gets angry, they should call this number.

7. The winners were him and his uncle.

8. I heard that you and they know the answer.

9. Some congressmen have lost your campaigns by ignoring public opinion.

10. Could anyone not enjoy her and Marcy's company?

11. Braswell learned faster than him.

12. John gambled that there was no love lost between Nancy and myself.

13. However much people hate taxes, you must pay your fair share.

14. Not one of the players was allowed to give their opinion.

Copyright © 1992 by Harcourt Brace Jovanovich, Inc. All rights reserved.

15. They are going to prod theirselves and get the job done.

16. Francine, she can't lose weight.

17. Either Lori or Grandma is better than myself at cooking.

18. My husband enjoys movies more than I.

19. Grant sent copies of the negatives to himself at his own address.

20. Between Hubert and I there is a lot of affection.

Copyright © 1992 by Harcourt Brace Jovanovich, Inc. All rights reserved.

EXERCISE 20C

Part One   Complete the following sentences by adding a pronoun. Be sure your choice of pronoun agrees in number with its antecedent. Apply the rules of formal English usage. The first sentence has been done as an example.

1. Each member of the squad provided _____*her*_____ own lunch.

2. Each taxpayer should save _____ sales receipts for certain items.

3. No one knows the combination to _____ locker.

4. The car registration for each vehicle belongs in _____ glove compartment.

5. The issue between Hilda and _____ is who will go to the prom.

6. Those people gave the caged animals _____ freedom.

7. After someone loses _____ ticket, she can replace it at no cost.

8. No one at the protest had made _____ own banner.

9. When a citizen becomes a scofflaw, _____ risks a jail term.

10. The package came to the Johnsons and _____ .

11. Leila likes lollipops more than _____ .

12. Charley learned more about physics than _____ .

Copyright © 1992 by Harcourt Brace Jovanovich, Inc. All rights reserved.

Part Two   For each sentence below, write a second sentence containing at least two pronouns that refer to nouns or pronouns in the first sentence. Circle these pronouns. Employ formal usage. The first pair of sentences has been done as an example.

1. My sister is taking four college classes. (She) likes (her) math class best although (she) finds all of (them) interesting.

2. Any driver may make a mistake. _____

   _____

   _____

3. Your task is to sort these names according to each man's preference.

   _____

   _____

   _____

4. Those fans who bought passes have first choice of seats. _____

   _____

   _____

5. No one took his key from the Lost and Found. _____

   _____

   _____

6. Tourists should be very cautious on that bridge._____

   _____

   _____

Copyright © 1992 by Harcourt Brace Jovanovich, Inc. All rights reserved.

21

Order of Pronouns and Spelling of Possessives

Order of Pronouns

When you are referring to someone else and to yourself in the same sentence, mention the other person's name (or the pronoun that replaces the name) before you mention your own.

INCORRECT	*I* and Joan like to study together.
CORRECT	Joan and *I* like to study together.
INCORRECT	The class listened to *me* and him.
CORRECT	The class listened to him and *me*.

The construction is actually not a rule of grammar; rather, it is considered a matter of courtesy.

Possessive Pronouns

Here is a list of possessive pronouns that you have already studied. This time, look carefully at how they are spelled and punctuated.

	Singular	*Plural*
first person	my, mine	our, ours
second person	your, yours	your, yours
third person	his	their, theirs
	her, hers	
	its	

Possessive pronouns do *not* contain apostrophes.

INCORRECT   That idea was *her's*.
CORRECT   That idea was *hers*.

Be especially careful not to confuse the possessive pronoun *its* with the contraction *it's* (it is).

INCORRECT   The movie pleased *it's* audience.
CORRECT   The movie pleased *its* audience.

Another source of confusion is the apostrophe which indicates the omitted letters in contractions. For example, the apostrophe in *don't* represents the missing *o* from **do not.** Some contractions of pronouns and verbs have the same pronunciations as certain possessive pronouns. These pairs of words sound alike but differ in meaning. Don't confuse them in your writing.

who's–whose
   Who's he? = *Who is* he?
   Whose seat is this? (possessive)
you're–your
   You're the winner. = *You are* the winner.
   It is *your* turn. (possessive)
they're–their
   They're leaving. = *They are* leaving.
   Their entry was selected. (possessive)

Circle the pronoun that correctly completes each sentence.

This coin is (yours, your's).

(Whose, Who's) your friend?

The bank just raised (its, it's) fees.

I don't know (whose, who's) car that is.

(Your, You're) luck has run out.

The new baby is (theirs, their's).

A final note: When you do pronoun exercises, or when you use pronouns in your own writing, remember to apply the rules. If you rely only on what "sounds right," your ear will usually supply only those pronouns that are appropriate in *informal* English.

EXERCISE 21A

If a sentence contains an error in pronoun usage, cross out the incorrect pronoun, and write in the correct form. Some sentences may contain more than one error. If a sentence contains no pronoun errors, label it *C* for *correct*. Apply the rules of formal English usage.

1. Their always making noise over there in there apartment.

2. Please leave the keys to the car for me and John.

3. After you eat, remember it's your turn to clean up.

4. They need to know whose car that is.

5. Its sure to be a battle when it's clear who's fault it was.

6. This suitcase is your's if there's a dent on the top.

7. Their never there when you need them.

8. I and Mickey get along very well.

9. Since its your pet, you should clean up its messes.

10. Our grandfather wired me and Pam the money.

11. Your over the weight limit for the job description as its spelled out on this form.

12. Send the invoice to me and Ronnie if you're not going to pay it.

Copyright © 1992 by Harcourt Brace Jovanovich, Inc. All rights reserved.

EXERCISE 21B

If a sentence contains an error in pronoun usage, cross out the incorrect pronoun, and write in the correct form. Some sentences may contain more than one error. If a sentence contains no pronoun errors, label it *C* for *correct*. Apply the rules of formal English usage.

1. Has anyone in the class done your homework?

2. These notebooks may be Jim's, or, maybe, there your's.

3. We players were told to keep the plan a secret between the coach and ourselves.

4. If your counselor gives you bad advice, its your right to question their judgment.

5. The rest of the cheesecake was divided between me and Patrick.

6. Polly and me know whose bike that was.

7. Members who bring guests should know their names, and you should introduce them to other members.

8. If you haven't lost your marbles, you're never too old to learn.

9. If a tourist goes to Hawaii, their better off skipping Honolulu with its freeways and skyscrapers.

10. The theater will be jammed, but Bonnie and myself know someone whose got front row seats for us and them.

Copyright © 1992 by Harcourt Brace Jovanovich, Inc. All rights reserved.

11. Its true that Xavier and her are alike, but after all, they're related.

12. Anybody who needs your form signed should get their early for their appointment.

Copyright © 1992 by Harcourt Brace Jovanovich, Inc. All rights reserved.

Pronoun Usage
Unit Review

Part One   Some of the following sentences contain pronoun errors. Cross out the incorrect pronouns, and write in the correct forms. If a sentence contains no pronoun errors, label it *C* for *correct*. Apply the rules of formal English usage.

1. It's a cinch that house is not their's.

2. Whose rights are being ignored?

3. I and Leona left it at their house.

4. Passengers need to have they're boarding passes handy if your not going to hold up the line.

5. Anyone who gets injured should go immediately to her supervisor.

6. Nobody on this block neglects their yard or allows their kids to run wild.

7. John Wilson and his wife Nelda lost their dog, but its been found by someone whose always kind to animals.

8. Ralphie and me knew the presents were for myself and him.

9. The news of their marriage surprised Mel more than me.

10. Patty left a ceramic pot which she herself had made in night school.

11. My sister is smarter than I, but I am stronger than her.

12. Someone whose refund is late should report your problem before its time for another payment.

Copyright © 1992 by Harcourt Brace Jovanovich, Inc. All rights reserved.

Part Two   Correct any pronoun errors that you find in the following paragraphs. Apply the rules of formal English usage.

I have a stepsister who's father married my mother after her divorce from my natural father. My mother's and stepfather's marriage is now a happy one, but their were times last year when my stepsister and me drove them nuts.

The problem was that Ellie, my stepsister, and myself are exactly the same age. If someone moves into your family, its better if they are much younger or much older. Me and Ellie were supposed to share everything, our room, our clothes, everything. Well, their isn't anything more hateful to twelve-year-olds than sharing.

Last month when she said, "That red skirt is mine not your's!" I slapped her, and she slapped me right back. I and she haven't spoken since, and we have a rope dividing that room of our's. She knows she'd better stay on her side of the rope, and that goes for anyone who visits her. They'd better stay in her territory too. Our parents have decided to leave me and her alone to settle this ourselfs. Its all right by me. This seems to be the best way for her and myself to get along.

Copyright © 1992 by Harcourt Brace Jovanovich, Inc. All rights reserved.

UNIT SIX

CAPITALIZATION, MORE PUNCTUATION, PLACEMENT OF MODIFIERS, PARALLEL STRUCTURE, AND IRREGULAR VERBS

22

Capitalization

The general principle behind capitalization is that **proper nouns** (names of *specific* persons, places, or things) are capitalized. **Common nouns** (names of *general* persons, places, or things) are *not* capitalized.

Study the following sentences, each of which illustrates a rule of capitalization.

1. Capitalize all parts of a person's name.

Sandra Day O'Connor is the highest ranking woman judge.

2. Capitalize the titles of relatives only when the titles precede the person's name or when they take the place of a person's name.

*A*unt Louise is a good friend.
Happy birthday, *M*other.
       but
My *u*ncle and my *m*other are both retired.

The same rule applies to professional titles.

> I visited *D*r. Wilson at his office.
> > but
> A *d*octor must study for many years before practicing.

3. Capitalize the names of streets, cities, and states.

> My uncle lives at 326 *W*right *S*treet, *L*oganville, *O*hio.

4. Capitalize the names of countries, languages, and ethnic groups.

> The *L*atvians of *R*ussia speak *R*ussian, but they are trying to get their own language of *L*atvian legalized.

5. Capitalize the names of specific buildings, geographical features, schools, and other institutions.

> We visited the *E*mpire *S*tate *B*uilding, *C*entral *P*ark, *C*olumbia *U*niversity, and the *G*uggenheim *M*useum.

6. Capitalize the days of the week, the months of the year, and the names of holidays. Do *not* capitalize the names of the seasons of the year.

> We usually celebrate *T*hanksgiving on the last *T*hursday in *N*ovember. I like to see the leaves change color in *a*utumn.

7. Capitalize directions of the compass only when they refer to specific regions.

> Just when she became used to the warm winters of the *S*outhwest, her company transferred her *n*orth to Minneapolis.

8. Capitalize the names of companies and brand names but not the names of the products themselves.

> Only the *C*oca-*C*ola *C*ompany can legally manufacture the base for the *s*oft *d*rink Coca-Cola.
> She uses nothing but *T*ide *s*oap.

9. Capitalize the first word of every sentence.

10. Capitalize the subject pronoun *I*.

11. Capitalize the first word of a title and all other words in the title except for articles (*a, an, the*) and except for conjunctions and prepositions that have fewer than five letters.

Who wrote *The Truth about Inflation?*
She sang, "*America the Beautiful.*"

12. Capitalize the names of academic subjects only if they are already proper nouns or if they are common nouns followed by a course number.

I am taking *S*panish, a *h*istory class, and *M*ath 101.

13. Capitalize the names of specific historical events, such as wars, revolutions, religious and political movements, and specific eras.

The *V*ietnam *W*ar, in which the United States sided with South Vietnam, ended in 1975.
During the *G*reat *D*epression, which lasted from 1929 to the early 1940s, many banks failed, and millions of Americans lost their jobs.
The *M*iddle *A*ges, a long period of European history, began with the *F*all of *R*ome in the fifth century and lasted for a thousand years until the *R*enaissance.

EXERCISE 22A

Add capital letters to the following sentences wherever they are necessary.

1. linda doesn't want to go to mexico because she doesn't speak spanish, but i assured her i had made an *a* in conversational spanish 300.

2. if you visit the nation's capital, be sure to drive down the potomac river to mount vernon, george washington's home and now a well-maintained historic site.

3. when my relatives from ontario, canada, visited us last october we took them to disneyland on cousin danny's birthday.

4. yes, teresa is a doctor, but she is a ph.d, not an m.d., and she is a physicist, not a physician.

5. when you drive west on interstate 10 through oklahoma, new mexico, and arizona, at times you'll cross the historic santa fe trail and also the famous highway 66.

6. ronald spent christmas day reading charles dickens' "a christmas carol" because he, ronald, admires the character scrooge, but he hates the happy ending.

7. my grandfather ike married my grandmother when she was eighteen; they were married on new year's day.

Copyright © 1992 by Harcourt Brace Jovanovich, Inc. All rights reserved.

8. when the united nations coalition went to war in the middle east in january of 1991 against iraq, that war pitted an arab country against most of the nations of the arab league.

9. francine was able to buy george orwell's novel *animal farm* at smith's bookstore on main street; it's for her brother, ned, whose birthday is on the fourth of april.

10. My aunt dolorosa is a practical joker; when i took my boyfriend sammy to the senior prom, she gave me a corsage, a Venus' flytrap, and for our wedding, auntie paid the organist to switch "the wedding march" from *Lohengrin* to cole porter's "begin the beguine."

Copyright © 1992 by Harcourt Brace Jovanovich, Inc. All rights reserved.

EXERCISE 22B

Add capital letters to the following sentences wherever they are necessary.

My final exam period last spring was more than usually hectic.

On january 20, i received a letter from my high school girlfriend lola in kansas city telling me that she had enjoyed my company so much at christmas vacation that she would arrive here at carson college the following monday. Well, not only did i have my roughest exam, english with mr. chamberlain, on monday, but that day was also my other girlfriend's birthday. Her name was leila, and I had never told lola about leila, or leila about lola. leila was expecting me to take her on monday to our favorite restaurant, charley's chowder and chili house.

I met lola at the airport, took her to the traveler's nook motel so she could rest, and rushed off to take my exam from mr. chamberlain. leila was also in that english class, and after the exam, she was expecting to study with me for our next exam, u.s. history 101 with dr. smith, but i told her i thought i was having a recurrent fever. (She knew i had contracted the disease coliform enteritis when i was in

Copyright © 1992 by Harcourt Brace Jovanovich, Inc. All rights reserved.

the peace corps in africa.) I rushed off to lola at the motel and said to her, "honey, I've got that african fever again. why don't you go shopping at the brentwood mall while i take some tylenol or aspirin and try to get a nap?"

lola left reluctantly for the mall, while i tried, unsuccessfully, to sleep. I was supposed to take both of them out for dinner at two different restaurants and study all night!

When lola returned, we went next door to delgado's hacienda where I ate three tacos and drank seven budweisers. I left lola back at the motel, telling her I had to study, and rushed off to take leila to charley's for her birthday dinner, where i drank several becks beers and ate too much german chocolate cake. then we went back to the motel, stopping on the way for a bottle of pepto-bismol. after a sleepless night, i got up to take lola to the airport and meet leila at the history exam.

when i put lola on the plane she whispered, "tony, christmas vacation was so special. i think you should sign up for a parenting class for the spring semester."

since then my life has gone rapidly downhill.

Copyright © 1992 by Harcourt Brace Jovanovich, Inc. All rights reserved.

EXERCISE 22C

Some capitalization rules include exceptions to the rule. For each of the rules listed below, write one sentence of your own that illustrates both the rule *and* its exception.

1. The rule about the names of academic subjects:

_____

_____

2. The rule about directions of the compass:

_____

_____

3. The rule about the titles of relatives:

_____

_____

4. The rule about words in the title of a book, movie, television program, and so on:

_____

_____

5. The rule about companies and brand names:

_____

_____

Copyright © 1992 by Harcourt Brace Jovanovich, Inc. All rights reserved.

6. The rule about periods of time, such as days of the week, months of the year:

_____

_____

7. The rule about professional titles:

_____

_____

Copyright © 1992 by Harcourt Brace Jovanovich, Inc. All rights reserved.

23

More on Punctuation

We learned in Lesson 11 to put a comma after an introductory dependent clause. At certain other times it is customary to separate **introductory** material from an independent clause which follows it.

> *According to the latest research*, your answer is correct. (introductory prepositional phrase)
> *Sliding across home plate*, he scored the winning run. (introductory participial phrase)

It is also customary to separate coordinate adjectives modifying the same noun. (Adjectives are *coordinate* if you can substitute *and* for the comma.)

> Mary is a happy, thoughtful person.
> or
> Mary is a happy *and* thoughtful person.

We learned in earlier lessons to use commas to set off appositives and parenthetical expressions. However, when the writer wishes to emphasize the importance or abruptness of such words, a **dash** may be used.

Nat loved only one person—himself.
Patty won—would you believe it?—six times in a row.

The **colon** is sometimes confused with the semicolon because of the similarity in names, but the two marks function differently. In addition to the colon's mechanical use to separate hours from minutes (8:45) and chapters from verses (*Genesis* 2:5), this mark is used frequently to introduce lists, summaries, series, and quotations which may be of almost any length or form. (Notice that what follows the **colon** is not necessarily an independent clause, that is, it may be fragmentary.)

Janey's backpack contained everything she would need for the hike: suntan lotion, a first aid kit, a bathing suit and towel, and a snack.
The secret to success in retailing may be summed up in three words: *location, location, location.*
Shakespeare said it so well: "Ripeness is all."

For an example of a colon introducing a summary, see p. 134.
An **apostrophe** with an *s* (*'s* or *s'*) on nouns and indefinite pronouns makes those words possessive. For most singular nouns or indefinite pronouns add the apostrophe followed by *s*.

Jill*'s* hair
the boy*'s* appearance
someone*'s* bicycle
John*'s* and Mary*'s* lunch

But if the singular noun ends in an *s*, *sh*, or a *z* sound, add either the apostrophe alone or an apostrophe and another *s*.

Le*s'* book or Les*'s* book
jazz*'* origins or jazz*'s* origins

For most plural nouns (those ending in an *s*, *sh*, or *z* sound), use the apostrophe alone.

the Joneses*'* car
the cats*'* fights
the ladies*'* dresses

But for a plural noun not ending in an *s*, *sh*, or *z* sound, add *'s*.

the children*'s* laughter

Sometimes possession is indicated by both the apostrophe and *of* in a preposi-tional phrase.

That book *of* Tom*'s* is over here.

And a possessive may follow the word it modifies.

Is this book Tom*'s*?

Direct quotations make writing vivid. Long direct quotations as in research papers, are indented and single spaced, but most direct quotes are simply enclosed in **quotation marks.**

"Come inside and have some coffee."

If the quotation is part of a longer sentence, it is set off by commas.

She said, "Come inside and have some coffee."
"I know," said the old man, "that you want me to go."

Three rules govern the use of quotation marks with other forms of punctuation:

1. The comma and period are *always* enclosed within quotation marks.

    "I like you," she said, "but I don't love you."

2. The colon and semicolon are *never* enclosed within quotation marks.

    He tried to sing, "Chloe"; but he didn't know the words.

3. Question marks, exclamation marks, and dashes are *within* the quotation marks if they apply to the quoted material and *after* the quotation marks if they apply to the whole sentence.

"Is he your friend?" Matt asked.
Did Matt say, "It's time to eat"?

You may have noticed in the discussion of capitalization that some titles are shown between quotation marks: "America the Beautiful," and some titles are shown in italics: *The Truth about Inflation*. The choice between these two ways to indicate titles is generally based on the length of the work so titled. The titles of minor works such as songs, short poems and stories, essays and articles in periodicals, and episodes of a series are put between **quotation marks.** The titles of longer works, and complete volumes or complete series are put in **italics.**

Italics are a special slanted typeface used by printers. In the handwritten and typewritten papers of most students, italics must be indicated by *underlining*.

I photocopied Frost's poem, "Birches" from *The Complete Poems of Robert Frost*.
See the chapter "Genetics" in the text *Modern Biology*.
One of her sources was the article, "Women at Work" in the *New York Times*.
They sang the duet "People Will Say We're in Love" from *Oklahoma*.

EXERCISE 23A

Add commas, colons, dashes, quotation marks, apostrophes, and italics to the following sentences wherever they are necessary. (Indicate italics by *underlining*.)

1. She lived by one rule Stand by your friends.

2. I like your speed said Coach Williams but can you play with a team?

3. The horses leg was broken so we had to put The Fastest Horse Alive asleep.

4. At midnight Johnny sang Auld Lang Syne and then the band played my favorite song Always.

5. We read the short story Good Country People from The Collected Works of Flannery O'Connor.

6. The teacher said Students I want you to see the film M.A.S.H. this weekend.

7. She inquired Have you read the article No More Losers in yesterdays Wall Street Journal?

8. The president reminded us of F.D.R.s famous line: We have nothing to fear but fear itself.

9. I love the song As Time Goes By in the movie Casablanca and also the line at the end This could be the beginning of a beautiful friendship.

Copyright © 1992 by Harcourt Brace Jovanovich, Inc. All rights reserved.

10. The sign said No Parking but I was driving my big brothers car so I parked.

11. At the beginning of Melvilles novel Moby Dick the narrator says Call me Ishmael.

12. According to Rick Olson no one can succeed without two qualities courage and persistence.

13. Leave me alone the hostess cried so all the guests marched out to the strains of Anchors Aweigh.

14. After I picked up my Sunday New York Times I read a review of the film Mermaids in the column Whats New in Cinema?

Copyright © 1992 by Harcourt Brace Jovanovich, Inc. All rights reserved.

EXERCISE 23B

Add capital letters, commas, dashes, apostrophes, colons, periods, quotation marks, and italics to the following sentences wherever they are necessary. (Indicate italics by *underlining*.)

1. according to dr nutley the humanoid which escaped from his lab was a harmless vegetarian with an addiction for diet cokes and prestone anti-freeze

2. luanda kissed her sister nellie goodbye handed her a copy of the bible, and said see you christmas eve sis

3. arturo naranjo could not dance but he took mrs. diazs class ballroom dancing so he could salsa and tango with estella santiago on cinco de mayo

4. we tried levelor blinds that we had purchased at sears but finally decided to leave the windows alone and instead planted outside a screen of nandina domestica.

5. his fender guitar boomed out six thirty-two bars of her favorite song born in the u s a

6. when mabel said maybe instead of saying i do to the ministers question melvin the groom was astonished and his mother mrs. mankiewizc was so angry she stalked down the aisle and drove away in the mercedes convertible she had planned to present to mabel as a wedding present

Copyright © 1992 by Harcourt Brace Jovanovich, Inc. All rights reserved.

7. the article no more oil originally appeared in the st louis dispatch on may 3 1990 and was reprinted in dr moores book middle east policy published by tempo publishing company

8. she came to her medical exam with the items specified in dr. nelsons directions a change of clothing a pair of bedroom slippers and a list of her allergies

9. my girlfriend naomi knows i like to eat puerto rican food so she went to morenos market and bought all the ingredients including many shipped fresh from the carribean

10. lionel entered the third annual young playwrights contest with his three-act play no time for love.

Copyright © 1992 by Harcourt Brace Jovanovich, Inc. All rights reserved.

24

Misplaced and Dangling Modifiers

Modifiers are words that are used to describe other words in a sentence. A modifier may be a single word, a phrase, or a clause. (Adjective clauses are discussed in Lesson 14.) Examples of some of the more common types of modifiers are given below. Circle the word that each italicized modifier describes.

ADJECTIVE	The dancer wore a *red* dress.
ADJECTIVE CLAUSE	The woman *who is speaking* is the chairperson.
PREPOSITIONAL PHRASE	The book *on the table* is my text.

The words you should have circled are *dress*, which is modified by ''red,'' *woman*, which is modified by ''who is speaking,'' and *book*, which is modified by ''on the table.''

Another type of modifier is a **participial phrase.** A participial phrase begins with a participle. A **participle** is a verb form that functions as an adjective. There are two kinds of participles. **Present participles** are formed by adding

-ing to the main verb (for example, *walking, knowing, seeing.*) **Past participles** are the verb forms that are used with the helping verb *have* (have *walked*, have *known*, have *seen*). Circle the word that each of the following participial phrases modifies.

Knowing the answer, Rebecca raised her hand.

A movie *directed by this man* has won an Oscar.

The words that you should have circled are *Rebecca* and *movie*.

If you look back at all the words that you have circled so far in this lesson, you will notice that although modifiers sometimes precede and sometimes follow the words they describe, they are in all cases placed as close as possible to the word that they describe. Failure to place a modifier in the correct position in a sentence results in an error known as a **misplaced modifier.**

MISPLACED	Ray bought a hamburger for his friend *with lots of onions.* (Does Ray's friend have lots of onions?)
CORRECT	Ray bought a hamburger *with lots of onions* for his friend.
MISPLACED	They gave an award to the athlete *plated with gold.* (Was the athlete plated with gold?)
CORRECT	They gave a trophy *plated with gold* to the athlete.

Correct the misplaced modifiers in the following sentences.

We used a poster for the dance painted in blues and greens.

Jack purchased his boat from a dealer that had a rebuilt engine.

I gave a party for my friend that will never be forgotten.

An error related to the misplaced modifier is the **dangling modifier.** A dangling modifier sometimes occurs when a participial phrase is placed at the beginning of a sentence. A participial phrase in this position *must describe the subject of the following clause.* If the subject of the clause cannot logically perform the action described in the participial phrase, the phrase is said to "dangle" (to hang loosely, without a logical connection).

DANGLING	*After leaving here,* his troubles lessened. (This sentence suggests that his *troubles* left here.)

CORRECT	After *he* left here, his troubles lessened.
DANGLING	*While laughing at me,* Sam's pants fell off. (This sentence suggests that Sam's *pants* were laughing.)
CORRECT	While *Sam* was laughing at me, his pants fell off.

Notice that there are several ways to correct dangling modifiers. You may add a noun or pronoun to the sentence to provide a word that the modifier can logically describe, or you may reword the entire sentence. *However, simply reversing the order of the dangling modifier and the rest of the sentence does not correct the error.*

DANGLING	When smiling, her teeth sparkle.
STILL DANGLING	Her teeth sparkle when smiling.
CORRECT	When she is smiling, her teeth sparkle.

Revise the following sentences so that they no longer contain dangling modifiers.

Driving down the street, Larry's car struck a lamppost.

Waiting for a promotion, his job drove him crazy.

While listening to the radio, my foot fell asleep.

When feeling happy, her future looks bright.

Because misplaced and dangling modifiers create confusing and even absurd sentences, you should be careful to avoid them in your writing.

EXERCISE 24A

Part One Construct five sentences of your own, using the modifiers listed below at the beginning of your sentences. Make certain that your modifiers do not dangle.

1. Not feeling which side was up, _____

   _____

2. After tasting nine pies, _____

   _____

3. By taking the easy path, _____

   _____

4. In order to insure a fair verdict, _____

   _____

5. When touching that coin, _____

   _____

6. Losing your way and tripping in the dark _____

   _____

Part Two Rewrite any sentences that contain a dangling or misplaced modifier. Some sentences need no change.

7. Moe gave a yell to his buddy that echoed in the room._____

   _____

8. They go to the movies on rainy days that win Academy Awards.

   _____

   _____

Copyright © 1992 by Harcourt Brace Jovanovich, Inc. All rights reserved.

9. When reading the book, his attention wandered. _____

_____

10. Knowing the lines by heart, we spoke them clearly. _____

_____

11. We gave a surprise to the chief that we sealed with Scotch tape.

_____

_____

12. After setting the table, the spoons were added. _____

_____

13. Once spilt, you must leave the milk alone and you must not cry.

_____

_____

14. Eager to rob the bank, a sudden siren changed all our plans.

_____

_____

15. When told a lie, Sally's reaction was disbelief. _____

_____

16. Reacting like a baby, my father made a face at me. _____

_____

Copyright © 1992 by Harcourt Brace Jovanovich, Inc. All rights reserved.

EXERCISE 24B

Some of the following sentences contain misplaced modifiers or dangling modifiers. Rewrite these sentences. If a sentence is correctly constructed, label it *C* for *correct*.

1. When fixing this recipe, your dishes must be clean.

   _____

   _____

2. Not having paid any rent for three months, she must borrow funds or lose her apartment.

   _____

   _____

3. He sent hundreds of cards to the friends that he had stamped.

   _____

   _____

4. Smiling at his famous wife, the actor signed his autograph.

   _____

   _____

5. To be rejected by that college, low grades and low scores on the entrance tests are a necessity.

   _____

   _____

Copyright © 1992 by Harcourt Brace Jovanovich, Inc. All rights reserved.

6. Martha located the street looking at the map.

_____

_____

7. Instead of eating lemon chiffon pie, a German chocolate cake was served.

_____

_____

8. While watching the TV show, the family cheered the contestant that lived next door.

_____

_____

9. To close a checking account, fill out the proper form.

_____

_____

10. He asked for a tie that was decorated with a hesitation in his manner.

_____

_____

11. Feeling the pain of the burn, he swabbed his arm with medicine.

_____

_____

12. He remembered the day that he had stroked Janis with a shovel in his hand.

_____

_____

Copyright © 1992 by Harcourt Brace Jovanovich, Inc. All rights reserved.

25

Parallel Structure

The term **parallel structure** means that similar ideas should be expressed in similar grammatical structures. For example, Benjamin Franklin quoted the following proverb:

Early to bed and early to rise make a man healthy, wealthy, and wise.

This proverb is a good illustration of parallel structure. It begins with two similar phrases, ''early to bed'' and ''early to rise,'' and it ends with a series of three similar words (they are all adjectives): *healthy, wealthy,* and *wise.*

In contrast, the following two versions of the same proverb contain some words that are *not* parallel.

Early to bed and early *rising* make a man healthy, wealthy, and wise.
Early to bed and early to rise make a man healthy, wealthy, and *give wisdom.*

Therefore, these last two sentences are *not* properly constructed.

Since there are many different grammatical structures in the English language, the possibilities for constructing non-parallel sentences may appear to be almost unlimited. Fortunately, you do not have to be able to identify all the grammatical structures in a sentence in order to tell whether or not that sentence has parallel structure. Sentences that lack parallel structure are usually so awkward that they are easy to recognize.

NOT PARALLEL   I enjoy *swiming, surfing,* and *to sail.*
PARALLEL   I enjoy *swimming, surfing,* and *sailing.*
NOT PARALLEL   The doctor told me *to stay* in bed, *that I should drink* lots of liquids, and *to take* two aspirins every four hours.
PARALLEL   The doctor told me *to stay* in bed, *to drink* lots of liquids, and *to take* two aspirins every four hours.
NOT PARALLEL   He wrote *quickly, carefully,* and *with clarity.*
PARALLEL   He wrote *quickly, carefully,* and *clearly.*

Revise each of the following sentences so that it is parallel in structure.

Potatoes can be boiled, baked, or you can fry them.

The movie was a success because of its good acting, interesting plot, and

its special effects were exciting.

Please list your name, how old you are, and your birthplace.

The Admissions Office told me to read the college catalog and that I should

make an appointment with a counselor.

Some errors in parallel structure occur when a writer is not careful in the use of correlative conjunctions. **Correlative conjunctions** are conjunctions that occur in pairs, such as:

both . . . and
either . . . or
neither . . . nor
not only . . . but also

Since these conjunctions occur in pairs, they are usually used to compare two ideas. For example:

Her workout was *neither* tedious *nor* tiring.

Correctly used, correlative conjunctions will structure a sentence in effective parallel form.

The rule for using correlative conjunctions is that the conjunctions *must be placed as close as possible to the words that are being compared.* For example:

I will choose *either* the yellow shirt *or* the green one.

not

I *either* will choose the yellow shirt *or* the green one.

Study the following examples of correctly and incorrectly placed correlative conjunctions.

INCORRECT You *not only* need to see a doctor *but also* a lawyer.
CORRECT You need to see *not only* a doctor *but also* a lawyer.
INCORRECT She *both* speaks French *and* Italian.
CORRECT She speaks *both* French *and* Italian.

Correct the misplaced correlative conjunctions in the following sentences.

He will go neither with his mother or stay with his sister.

These old chairs both are comfortable and durable.

They not only traveled to the moon but also on to Jupiter.

You either ought to see less of her or marry her.

EXERCISE 25A

Rewrite any sentences that lack parallel structure. If a sentence is already parallel, label it *C* for *correct*.

1. Manny was very smart, had a lot of knowledge, and was full of courage.

_____

_____

2. After you eat one of Paula's dinners, you will want to be without your jacket, not have your belt tight, and get a short nap.

_____

_____

_____

3. She was both tall for her age and someone who knew how to wear attractive clothes.

_____

_____

4. They not only washed the dishes but also the silver.

_____

_____

5. His rendition of ''Stardust'' was well received by the audience and the critics liked it too.

_____

_____

_____

Copyright © 1992 by Harcourt Brace Jovanovich, Inc. All rights reserved.

6. Clean the vegetables, slice them, and drop them into boiling water.

_____

_____

7. A jerk has no self-awareness or is a type of fool.

_____

_____

8. He was neither a lover nor would he even talk to girls.

_____

_____

9. His old car was economical, easily maintained, and very attractive.

_____

_____

10. She not only lost her cool but also the tennis match too.

_____

_____

11. I either will leave late Tuesday night or early Wednesday morning.

_____

_____

12. My modeling coach advised me to shorten my hair, that I should lose at least twelve pounds and sent me to buy my clothes from "Gianna's."

_____

_____

_____

Copyright © 1992 by Harcourt Brace Jovanovich, Inc. All rights reserved.

EXERCISE 25B

Rewrite any sentences that lack parallel structure or that contain misplaced or dangling modifiers. If a sentence needs no revision, label it *C* for *correct*.

1. Feeling her way in the dark, the furniture presented many obstacles.

_____

_____

2. To enter the contest, the entry forms must be carefully completed by each contestant.

_____

_____

3. Repairing the engine in fifteen minutes, Pete proved to us that he was a first-class mechanic.

_____

_____

4. We received colorful Christmas neckties from distant relatives that had been hand painted.

_____

_____

5. Her old dog, not knowing any new tricks, showed us his old tricks.

_____

_____

Copyright © 1992 by Harcourt Brace Jovanovich, Inc. All rights reserved.

6. Leaving out most of the answers, the questions were answered by Angela in several minutes.

_____

_____

7. Quincey wasted no time on trashy movies, and he watched no trashy TV either.

_____

_____

8. The coach wanted fast players who were aggressive and they wouldn't be bothered either by the fans.

_____

_____

9. Admired by every boy in the class, Valerie accepted their admiration as a tribute to her looks, the charm that she possessed, and her facility with words.

_____

_____

10. Mrs. Wilson planned for her children to be good students and their graduation would be with honors.

_____

_____

11. Relaxed and confident, John shot baskets and made free throws with ease.

_____

_____

Copyright © 1992 by Harcourt Brace Jovanovich, Inc. All rights reserved.

26

Irregular Verbs

Verbs have three **principal** (meaning "most important") **parts:** the *present* (which, when preceded by *to,* becomes the *infinitive*), the *past,* and the *past participle.*

The **present** form may stand alone as a main verb without any helping verb. For example:

I *live* in California.
Many students *ride* the bus to school.

It may also be preceded by a helping verb, such as *can, could, do, does, did, may, might, must, shall, should, will,* or *would.* (A list of helping verbs appears in Lesson 4, p. 38.)

John *should see* a doctor.
She *may need* a new car.

However, the present form is *not* used after any forms of the helping verbs *have (has, have, had)* or *be (am, is, are, was, were, been).*

The **past** form is used alone as a main verb. It is *not* preceded by a helping verb when expressing the simple past tense.

Our friends *left* town yesterday.
The class *began* twenty minutes ago.

The **past participle** is *always* preceded by at least one, and sometimes more than one, helping verb. The helping verb is often a form of *have* or *be*.

I *have washed* the car.
The vegetables *were grown* in our garden.

Most English verbs are regular. A **regular** verb forms both its past and past participle by adding -ed to the present. (If the present already ends in -e, only a -d is added.)

Present	*Past*	*Past Participle*
talk	talked	talked
like	liked	liked

Any verb that does *not* form both its past and past participle by adding -ed or -d is considered **irregular.** For example:

Present	*Past*	*Past Participle*
eat	ate	eaten
write	wrote	written
begin	began	begun

Study the sentences below. Notice that the differences between regular and irregular verbs are not apparent in the present tense and that, with regular verbs, the *past* and the *past participle* are spelled alike.

REGULAR   IRREGULAR

present tense

REGULAR	IRREGULAR
I *live* here.	I *eat* pizza.
I *walk* my dog.	I *am* a student.
We *rent* this place.	I *write* essays.
	We *begin* the project today.

(continued)

past tense

I *lived* here.

I *walked* my dog.

We *rented* this place.

I *ate* pizza.

I *was* a student.

I *wrote* essays.

We *began* the project yesterday.

present perfect tense (with past participle)

I *have lived* here.

I *have walked* my dog.

We *have rented* this place.

I *have eaten* pizza.

I *have been* a student.

I *have written* essays.

We *have begun* the project.

past perfect tense (with past participle)

I *had lived* here.

I *had walked* my dog.

We *had rented* this place.

I *had eaten* pizza before then.

I *had been* a student in 1987.

I *had written* essays before I knew her.

We *had begun* the project before the storm hit.

Since irregular verbs by definition have irregular spellings, you must *memorize* the spelling of their past and past participle forms. Irregular verbs include many of the most commonly used verbs in the English language (for example, *come, go, eat, drink, sit, stand*), so it is important to study them carefully.

Here is a list of some of the most commonly used irregular verbs. In addition to learning the verbs on this list, if you are not sure whether or not a verb is irregular, look it up in the dictionary. A good dictionary will list the principal parts of an irregular verb in addition to defining its meaning.

Present	Past	Past Participle			
beat	beat	beaten	bring	brought	brought
begin	began	begun	build	built	built
bend	bent	bent	buy	bought	bought
bleed	bled	bled	catch	caught	caught
blow	blew	blown	choose	chose	chosen
break	broke	broken	come	came	come

cut	cut	cut		read	read	read
do	did	done		ride	rode	ridden
draw	drew	drawn		ring	rang	rung
drink	drank	drunk		rise	rose	risen
drive	drove	driven		run	ran	run
eat	ate	eaten		see	saw	seen
fall	fell	fallen		sell	sold	sold
feed	fed	fed		send	sent	sent
feel	felt	felt		set	set	set
find	found	found		shake	shook	shaken
fly	flew	flown		shoot	shot	shot
freeze	froze	frozen		sing	sang	sung
get	got	got *or* gotten		sink	sank	sunk
give	gave	given		sit	sat	sat
go	went	gone		sleep	slept	slept
grow	grew	grown		speak	spoke	spoken
have	had	had		spend	spent	spent
hear	heard	heard		spin	spun	spun
hide	hid	hidden		stand	stood	stood
hit	hit	hit		steal	stole	stolen
hurt	hurt	hurt		stick	stuck	stuck
keep	kept	kept		swear	swore	sworn
know	knew	known		swim	swam	swum
lay	laid	laid		take	took	taken
leave	left	left		teach	taught	taught
lend	lent	lent		tear	tore	torn
lie	lay	lain		tell	told	told
lose	lost	lost		think	thought	thought
make	made	made		throw	threw	thrown
mean	meant	meant		wear	wore	worn
meet	met	met		weep	wept	wept
pay	paid	paid		win	won	won
put	put	put		write	wrote	written

Notice that compound verbs follow the same pattern as their root form. For example:

be*come*	be*came*	be*come*
for*give*	for*gave*	for*given*
under*stand*	under*stood*	under*stood*

EXERCISE 26A

Circle the verb form that correctly completes each sentence. If you are not absolutely certain of the correct form, go back to the list of irregular verbs *before* you make your choice.

1. Marla has (lended, lent) me her bike.

2. Have the new storms (brought, brung) rain?

3. Walter's company had (builded, built) six shopping centers.

4. Marcella (become, became) the first woman president of National Bank.

5. Has Shirley's little brother ever (ate, eaten) Belgian waffles?

6. The senator had (chosen, choosed) to run for reelection.

7. Marvin (spended, spent) his spare time in the library.

8. Have Aretha and Sammy (sang, sung) this number together in the past?

9. That little canary had (drunk, drank) every drop of lemonade.

10. In that war, the Air Force had (done, did) its best to avoid hitting civilian targets.

11. The driver that (wonned, won) the race was on TV.

12. The expedition was (drove, driven) crazy by mosquitoes in the swamps.

13. He (run, ran) the full gamut of his emotions from A to B.

14. They have (broken, broke) every record in the state.

Copyright © 1992 by Harcourt Brace Jovanovich, Inc. All rights reserved.

15. Had your older brother (teach, taught) you your times tables?

16. As the weeks passed they had (growed, grew, grown) fond of Nathaniel.

17. She has (gave, give, given) that same speech three times to great applause.

18. These eggs have been (lain, layed, laid) by free-ranging hens.

19. Malcolm (set, sat) with Irene in the corner booth.

20. The troops have (wore, worn) that emblem as a shield of honor.

21. Michael (meant, meaned) well, but he fouled up the new engine.

22. The P.O.W.'s have (hid, hidden) along the river.

23. The doctors say that she has (tore, torn) a ligament in her ankle.

24. The palomino had been (ridden, rode) hard and put away wet.

Copyright © 1992 by Harcourt Brace Jovanovich, Inc. All rights reserved.

Capitalization, More Punctuation,
Placement of Modifiers,
Parallel Structure, and Irregular Verbs
Unit Review

Part One Add any missing capitals, commas, quotation marks, apostrophes, or italics to the following paragraphs. Correct any misplaced or dangling modifiers, and restructure any faulty parallelism.

1. laurence olivier was probably britains and perhaps the worlds greatest actor. olivier a master of makeup was able to transform himself into hundreds of young or old masculine or feminine saintly devilish or ordinary human beings. in one play he was shakespeares vengeful brooding prince hamlet of denmark. in his next play he became the aged bumbling lecherous mr. shallow or became the very ordinary dr. astrov in the russian play uncle vanya by chekov. opposite marilyn monroe olivier played the serious good-hearted prince in the comic movie the prince and the showgirl. but in the film richard the third olivier became evil incarnate in the person of englands highly intelligent vastly evil crippled king. long before his death, olivier was made a real noble being knighted as sir laurence for his remarkable deeds.

2. some critics of people magazine say the weekly is nothing

Copyright © 1992 by Harcourt Brace Jovanovich, Inc. All rights reserved.

more than a glitzy gossip sheet pandering to the yuppie crowd that has flourished since the celebrity-conscious reagan era of the eighties. for example the january 21 1991 issue features on its cover a demure cher who says in a new book that her secret is a healthy life and not the surgeons knife. inside are stories about such celebrities as princess di of england who had recently run away from her bodyguards to mope alone and unguarded on a norfolk beach. defenders of the time and life publication point out three virtues of the weekly it satisfies in a harmless way the natural human craving for gossip; secondly it carries good serious reviews in its picks and pans columns on the current pop culture scene; and thirdly in its occasional lengthy reports of major human interest stories, such as that of christa mcauliffe one of the astronauts in the challenger disaster people demonstrates good solid journalism.

3.   inside each human are three people struggling for control. one of these people a good-goody wants that human to be an angel twenty-four hours a day. the goody-goody prizes respectability above all and like the biblical pharisee in the gospel story is sure he has a corner on goodness. another person inside us says i want what

Copyright © 1992 by Harcourt Brace Jovanovich, Inc. All rights reserved.

i want when i want it so stay out of my way. this cold proud tempter is called self. a third person within us is a sensible being who says try your best to be a decent person treating all your fellow humans with charity including yourself.

Part Two   Correct any improper verb forms in the following paragraphs.

Once a great king had three daughters. The oldest daughter Thika had ate nothing but peanut butter since she had began to talk. When she become married to the poor but handsome Prince of Krag and moved to his rocky kingdom, she finded that her new land had no peanut butter, not one glob. She rapidly losted weight and sunk into depression.

The second princess, Yuk, who ate nothing but oysters, moved to the mountains of Drek, where her poor husband's family had set upon the throne since time begun. When she learnt that Drek had no oysters, not even froze ones, she weeped and weeped. Soon she was just a shadow of her old self.

Sophia, the youngest daughter, had not ate anything since infancy. Instead she had drank the morning dew from posies, buttercups and other blossoms in her father's garden. When she moved with the Prince of Arida to his poverty-stricken desert kingdom, she

Copyright © 1992 by Harcourt Brace Jovanovich, Inc. All rights reserved.

soon beginned to shrivel like a leaf. She wanted to lay down and die. Sophia knowed her sisters must be suffering too, and she meaned to save herself and them. But how?

The answer come to her in a dream. As soon as she awaked, she arranged to meet her two sisters. "Sisters," said Princess Arida, "I dreamt about a country called Merrika, where all the people have been trying to lose weight, but most have never losted a single pound. We will sell these Merrikans morning dew from my country and oysters and peanuts from yours."

"But, sister," said the oldest princess, "You know peanuts and oysters are not to be found in our countries and morning dew has never been knowed in Arida."

"Exactly," said the youngest Princess, "that is why each container we sell will bore our slogan: **'There's nothing to it because it has no calories!'** The Merrikans will buy food with absolutely no calories by the carload."

And she was right. Each year since then Merrika has buyed tens of thousands of jars and bottles of Princess Products with nothing in them. The three princesses have growed old and fat on *real* oysters, peanut butter and morning dew which they have got with all their new wealth. And—they will live happily ever after.

Copyright © 1992 by Harcourt Brace Jovanovich, Inc. All rights reserved.

274

ANSWERS TO "A" EXERCISES

Exercise 1A

1. <u>Sir William Jones</u> <u><u>lived</u></u>
2. <u>He</u> <u><u>decided</u></u>
3. <u>Sanskrit</u> <u><u>was</u></u>
4. <u>Sir William</u> <u><u>made</u></u>
5. <u>Sanskrit</u> <u><u>resembled</u></u>
6. <u>India</u> <u><u>is</u></u>
7. <u>Europe</u> <u><u>was</u></u>
8. <u>words</u> <u><u>sounded</u></u>
9. <u>example</u> <u><u>is</u></u>
10. <u>word</u> <u><u>means</u></u>
11. <u>word</u> <u><u>is</u></u>
12. <u>(You)</u> <u><u>notice</u></u>
13. <u>*Matar*</u> <u><u>is</u></u>
14. <u>word</u> <u><u>is</u></u>

15. Jones discovered
16. He decided
17. explanation seemed
18. languages had
19. scholars confirmed
20. They called
21. Indo-European was
22. languages come
23. descendants include

Exercise 2A

1. Stress is
2. stress causes
3. changes seem
4. loss divorce loss are
5. tract is
6. stomachs ulcers disorders occur
7. women have / men become
8. problems occur become / someone loses separates
9. Stress triggers
10. you are / you ought
11. (You) think
12. (You) deal
13. (You) talk
14. (You) Listen / (you) avoid
15. (You) Use
16. you get / (you) begin
17. Nobody escapes / stress is / we face

Exercise 3A

1. babies join
2. members come
3. eyes are / it has
4. It knows / she uses
5. It clings goes

6. childhood extends
7. it stays / it begins
8. They chase pull play
9. games teach
10. fur collects
11. All like
12. monkeys groom
13. monkey is / mother adult comes
14. monkeys need

Exercise 4A

1. Rattlesnakes hunt
2. they can chew / they swallow
3. They lie
4. rattlesnake does see / it does have
5. organ lies
6. rattlesnake flicks / it retracts
7. organ collects
8. brain interprets knows
9. snake can strike shoot pull
10. animal will die / rattler begins
11. Rattlers do hunt
12. animals will eat / they strike
13. humans should be / they are walking

Exercise 5A

1. Smokers lose
2. smoking will cause
3. smoker faces
4. relatives friends wonder / smokers can continue
5. Smokers smoke / nicotine is
6. smokers begin / they are
7. They feel / they are going
8. Many smoke / smoking seems

9. they go / they realize
10. Four want / percent succeed
11. symptoms cause
12. Nicotine is / addicts can turn

Exercise 6A

1. live
2. quit
3. are
4. have
5. have
6. have
7. communicate
8. have
9. involves
10. are
11. show
12. are
13. mean

Exercise 7A

1. were
2. is
3. keep
4. has
5. live
6. Does
7. was
8. was
9. Has
10. is
11. were
12. are
13. are
14. do
15. has

16. was
17. run
18. are
19. is
20. is

Exercise 8A

1. makes
2. disagree
3. was
4. are
5. doesn't
6. is
7. has
8. are
9. is
10. was
11. insists
12. Does
13. was
14. has
15. were
16. was
17. is
18. Have

Exercise 9A

1. exists
2. has
3. damages
4. were
5. loses
6. Does
7. impresses
8. was
9. is
10. is

11. was
12. detract
13. are
14. keeps
15. appear
16. are
17. Do
18. have

Exercise 10A

Answers will vary.

Sample for 1–4: My aunt is a widow, but she has a busy social life.
Sample for 5–11: The dog is huge, but she's very gentle.
Sample for 12–15: The dog is huge; she is a St. Bernard dog.

or

The dog is huge; however, she is very gentle.

Exercise 11A

Answers will vary.

Sample for 1–6: Marie left early for work although it was still dark.
Sample for 7–11: He will go wherever you point your finger.
Sample for 12–16: Because Maria is an expert hairdresser, she will make you
look terrific.

Exercise 12A

Part One

1. (When) Leila calls Mitchell,   away, for

2. blushed, for her smile gave her away (even though) she tried to hide it.

3. off; however, the engine continued to run (because) it was so hot.

4. (If) she continues to set new sales records, she will be the new sales
manager; all of the employees would like that.

5. (after) the wind died, yet

6. (Although) her make up was smudged, no one noticed, and

7. rainstorm; no one cared (because) they were anxious to get started.

8. (Although) Leila is in kindergarten, she can do many first-grade skills, and she is strong like her dad.

9. Marie (because) her mother likes that name, and so does Leila.

10. woods; (when) they look out their windows, they see deer and wild turkeys.

Part Two

Answers will vary.

Sample answer: I love Wilma, but she doesn't love me because I am a gang member.

Exercise 13A

¶1 neighborhood, you may   and *ravens* because they are
family, called the corvids, and   [appositive, comes in Lesson 15]
¶2 blunt tip not pointed like   by their tails because a crow
¶3 are found throughout every part   earth from above the Arctic
of climate from frozen   and Africa and at the fringes
¶4 forth incessantly like a group   of teamwork among ravens
¶5 cultures because they scavenge

Exercise 14A

1. C
2. dictionary, don't
3. example, we
4. hand, the
5. are, in fact, an

Part Two

6. synonyms; that is, English
7. group, for example, have
8. However, as   *pig*, you
9. connotation; some
10. subject, and, as a result, shapes
11. advertisers are, of course, masters

12. shaped, I suppose, by   phrases, and
13. power; send

Exercise 15A

1. sister, a chef at a gourmet restaurant, is
2. Cooperstown, home of Baseball's Hall of Fame, is
3. C
4. teacher, Mr. Iglesias, changed
5. C
6. Ravin, my second cousin, came
7. name, poison ivy.
8. team, The
9. C
10. C
11. blue, or indigo, is
12. C
13. Edison, inventor of the electric light, conducted
14. detectives, sometimes called *private eyes*, lead
15. C
16. *lox*, that is, smoked

Exercise 16A

¶1 wife, who was gifted with common sense, said
¶2 food, which only humans do, is
¶3 liquid, which is usually water, transfers   dry-heat stage, which

Exercise 17A (Circled commas are optional.)

1. C
2. San Diego, California, and   Topeka, Kansas.
3. tall, quite blonde ⊙ and quite
4. C
5. Philadelphia, Pennsylvania
6. ceiling, arched right and left ⊙ and
7. C
8. C
9. July 4, 1776, or December 7, 1941.

10. London, England, should
11. lawyer, for a dentist⊙ and
12. *E, R*⊙ and
13. Suite 904 Tower Building, 303 Adams Street, Lindenville, Ohio 86929.
14. C
15. C

Exercice 18A

1. They wrote us
2. She gave you
3. They sent the pictures to her.
4. We relied on them
5. You liked him
6. She baked him
7. (No change)
8. They sought it
9. he
10. she (after linking verb)
11. he
12. they
13. she
14. us
15. him
16. him
17. us
18. them
19. she
20. us

Exercice 19A

1. she
2. me
3. he
4. her
5. I
6. me
7. they

8. she
9. himself
10. me
11. I
12. May be either *me* or *I* depending on context. Discuss in class.
13. he
14. we
15. themselves
16. me
17. herself
18. I
19. us
20. I

Exercise 20A

1. He
2. I
3. her
4. she
5. their
6. his
7. themselves
8. she
9. his
10. he
11. me
12. she
13. her
14. his   he
15. they

Exercise 21A

1. They're always making noise over there in their apartment.
2. for John and me
3. C
4. C

5. It's sure   whose
6. yours
7. They're never
8. Mickey and I
9. Since it's
10. Pam and me
11. You're over   as it's spelled
12. Ronnie and me

Exercise 22A

1. Linda   Mexico   Spanish   I   I   *A*   Conversational Spanish
2. If   Potomac River   Mount Vernon   George Washington's
3. When   Ontario, Canada   October   Disneyland   Cousin Danny's
4. Yes   Teresa   Ph.D   M.D.
5. When   Interstate   Oklahoma   New   Mexico   Arizona   Santa
   Fe Trail   Highway
6. Ronald   Christmas Day   Charles Dicken's   "A Christmas Carol"
   Ronald   Scrooge
7. My Grandfather Ike   New Year's Day
8. When   United Nation's Coalition   Middle East   January   Iraq
   Arab   Arab League
9. Francine   George Orwell's   *Animal Farm*   Smith's Bookstore
   Main Street   Ned   April
10. Aunt Dolorosa   I   Sammy   Senior Prom   Venus'   Auntie
   "The Wedding March"   Cole Porter's "Begin the Beguine"

Exercise 23

1. rule: Stand by your friends.
2. "I like your speed," said Coach Williams, "but can you play with a team?"
3. horse's   broken, so   "The Fastest Horse Alive"
4. "Auld Lang Syne," and then   song, "Always."
5. "Good Country People" *The Collected Works of Flannery O'Connor*.
6. said, "Students, I   the film *M.A.S.H.* this weekend."
7. inquired, "Have you read the article 'No More Losers' in yesterday's *Wall Street Journal*?" [Note that single quotation marks are used for a quotation within a quotation.]
8. line: "We have nothing to fear but fear itself."

9. song "As Time Goes By"   *Casablanca*
   end: "This could be the beginning of a beautiful friendship."
10. said, "No Parking," but   brother's car, so
11. Melville's   *Moby Dick*, the   says, "Call me Ishmael."
12. Olson, no one   qualities: courage and persistence.
13. "Leave me alone!" the hostess cried, so   of "Anchors Aweigh."
14. *New York Times,   Mermaids*   column "What's New in Cinema?"

Exercise 24A

Answers will vary.

Part One

Sample for 1–5: Not feeling which side was up, the skydiver twisted to look
at the sun.

Part Two

Sample for 7–16: To his buddy, Moe gave a yell that echoed in the room.

Exercise 25A

Answers will vary.

Samples:
1. Manny was very smart, knowledgeable, and courageous.
5. His rendition of "Stardust" was well received by the audience and by
   the critics.

Exercise 26A

1. lent
2. brought
3. built
4. became
5. eaten
6. chosen
7. spent
8. sung
9. drunk
10. done

11. won
12. driven
13. ran
14. broken
15. taught
16. grown
17. given
18. laid
19. sat
20. worn
21. meant
22. hidden
23. torn
24. ridden

Index

Academic subjects, capitalization of, 233
Actor-action patterns of sentences, 1–2
Adjective clause(s). *See* Nonrestrictive clauses;
  Restrictive clauses
Adjectives, 6
  each, every, or *any* used as, 87
  See also Indefinite adjectives
Adverb clause(s), 110–11
Adverbs, 4
And, subjects joined by, 87
Antecedent, 189
  pronouns agreeing in number with, 60–61,
    210–11
Any used as an adjective, 87
Apostrophes, possessive pronouns and, 222–23
Appositives, 157–60
  use of commas with, 158–60

Brand names, capitalization of, 232
Buildings, capitalization of names of, 232

Capitalization, 231–33
Clause(s), 109–11
  in compound sentences, conjunctions joining,
    16–17, 98
  punctuation of, 168–70
  See also Dependent clauses; Independent
    clauses; Nonrestrictive clauses; Restrictive
    clauses
Collective nouns, subject-verb agreement
  and, 80
Colon, 242
Comma splices, 123

Commands, subject pronoun of, 5
Commas
  in addresses, 179–80
  appositives and, 158–60
  in compound sentence joined by coordinating
    conjunction, 98–99
  in dates, 180
  dependent clauses and, 109
  in direct address, 148
  with *etc.,* 146
  independent clauses and, 98
  parenthetical expressions and, 145–47
  preceding coordinating conjunction, 98
  restrictive and nonrestrictive clauses and,
    167–70
  in series, 179
Common nouns, capitalization of, 231
Company names, capitalization of, 232
Comparisons, pronouns in, 201–202
Complement, subject-verb agreement and, 62
Complex sentences, 109–11
  adjective clauses and, 169–70
  changing run-on sentences to, 123
Compound-complex sentences, 121–22
Compound sentences, 97–102
  compared with complex sentences, 110
  parenthetical expressions joining clauses of,
    147
  changing run-on sentences to, 123
Condition conjunctions, 110
Conjunctions, 110
  joining two subjects, 87
  See also Coordinating conjunctions;
    Correlative conjunctions; Subordinating
    conjunctions

Coordinating conjunctions, 98–99
in run-on sentences, 121–23
use of commas with, 98–99
Correlative conjunctions, 258
Countries, capitalization of names of, 232

Dangling modifier, 250–51
Dash, 241
Dependent clauses, 109–11
as sentence fragments, 134
subordinating conjunctions and, 110
use of commas with, 111
· See also adverb clauses
Dependent phrases, as sentence fragments, 134–35
Direct address, punctuation of, 148
Directions of compass, capitalization of, 232

Each, used as adjective, 87
emphasis, personal pronouns ending in *-self* or *-selves* for, 203–204
Etc., punctuation of, 147
Ethnic groups, capitalization of names of, 232
Every, used as adjective, 87

First person, 213
Formal speech and writing, subject pronoun used for, 190–91

Gerund, 48

Helping verbs, 37–39
Here, questions and statements beginning with, 63–64
Holidays, capitalization of, 232

Indefinite pronouns, 71
agreement in number, 71
singular and plural verbs and, 72
Independent clauses, 98
and comma splices, 123
coordinating conjunction between, 98
and run-on sentences, 123
semicolon between, 99
use of commas with, 98
Indirect object, 191–92
Infinitive(s), 3
Informal speech, object pronouns in, 190–91
Interrupting expressions. *See* Parenthetical expressions
Introductory material, 241
Irregular verbs, 266–68
Italics, 244

Languages, capitalization of names of, 232

Main verbs, 37
Misplaced modifiers, 250
Modifiers, 249
dangling, 250
misplaced, 250
Months, capitalization of names of, 232
Myself, as subject or object pronoun, 203–204

Nonrestrictive clauses, punctuation of, 169
Nor
joining singular and plural subject, 88
joining two singular subjects, 88
Nouns, 4
appositives and, 157–58
plural in form and singular in meaning, 79–80
plurals of, 60
repeated in pronoun form, 203
showing possession, 6
used as object of preposition, 26
See also Collective nouns; Common nouns; Proper nouns

Object of preposition, 26
Object pronoun(s), 191–92
in comparisons, 202
plural, 190
singular, 189
used as indirect objects, 191
Or
joining singular and plural subject, 88
joining two singular subjects, 88
Ownership, possessive pronouns and, 191–92

Parallel structure, 257–58
Parenthetical expressions, 145
punctuation of, 145–48
Participial phrase, 249
Participles, 48, 249
Past participles, 49, 250, 266–68
Pattern of sentence, 15–16
Personal pronouns, ending in *-self* or *-selves* 203
Person, pronouns agreeing in, 213–14
Phrases, 98, 134–36
See also Participial phrase; Prepositional phrases
Place conjunctions, 110
Plural subjects, 59
Possessive pronouns, 6, 192–93, 222–23
plural, 190
singular, 189
spelling of, 222

Prepositional phrases, 26
  subject-verb agreement, 28
Prepositions, 25–26
  object pronouns after, 26
Present participles, 49, 249
Professional titles, capitalization of, 232
Pronouns, 5, 189–90
  agreement in number, 209–10
  agreement in person, 213
  in comparisons, 201–202
  doubling subjects and, 203
  order of, 221
  singular and plural, 203, 209
  See also Indefinite pronouns; Object
    pronouns; Possessive pronouns;
    Reflexive pronouns; Subject pronouns
Proper nouns, capitalization of, 231
Punctuation
  of addresses, 179–80
  of appositives, 158–59
  of clauses, 98, 109, 111
  of dates, 179–80
  of parenthetical expressions, 145–47
  of series, 179
  See also Capitalization; Commas; Semicolons

Questions
  beginning with *there* or *here*, subject-verb
    agreement in, 63–64
  and helping verbs, 38
  subject-verb order in, 63
Quotation marks, 243–44

Reason conjunctions, 110
Reflexive pronouns, 203–204
Relatives, capitalization of family titles of, 231
Restrictive clauses, commas and, 168
Run-on sentences, 123

-*s* added to nouns and verbs, 59–60
Seasons, capitalization of names of, 232
Second person, 213
-*self*, personal pronouns ending in, 203–204
-*selves*, personal pronouns ending in, 203–204
Semicolon
  joining independent clauses, 99
  parenthetical expressions joining clauses in
    compound sentences, 100–101
  run-on sentences and, 122–23

Sentence fragments, 133–35
Sentences
  actor-action pattern of, 1–2, 7
  complete, 1
  with inverted pattern, subject-verb agreement
    in, 63
  with parallel structure, 257–58
  patterns of, 15–17
  positions of helping verbs in, 38
  subject-verb core of, 2
  See also Run-on sentences
Shift in person, 213–14
Singular subjects, 4–5
Subject(s), 2
  in commands, 5
  of compound sentences, 16
  doubled, 203
  identification of, prepositional phrases and, 28
  singular and plural, 1–2, 15–16
Subject pronouns, 5, 190–91
  in comparisons, 201–202
  plural, 190
  singular, 189
Subject-verb agreement, 59–60, 62–63
Subordinating conjunctions, 110
  in run-on sentences, 122–23
  used to begin adverb clause, 110

Tense, 3
  helping verbs and, 38
Than and *then*, 201–202
There, questions and statements beginning with,
  subject-verb order in, 63
Third person, 213
Time conjunctions, 110
Titles, capitalization of, 233

Unit of time, weight, or measurement, 79

Verbal, 48
Verbs, 2–3
  agreement with subject, 59–60, 62–63
  of compound sentences, 205
  identification of, prepositional phrases and,
    28–29
  singular and plural, 61
  tense of, 3
  See also Helping verbs; Main verbs; Irregular
    verbs

A 1
B 2
C 3
D 4
E 5
F 6
G 7
H 8
I 9
J 0